# A REASON
# TO LOVE MORE

# A REASON TO LOVE MORE

## The Alzheimer's Enigma

# Anne Joyce

THREE SISTERS PRESS

Published by Three Sisters Press,
Co. Wexford

First published: 2016

Managing Editor: Michael Freeman

Editor: Helen Ashdown, Wordswork,
Clonleigh, Palace, Enniscorthy, Co. Wexford

First Draft Reviews: Margaret Hawkins, Ann C. Ashdown

Design and Layout: Rosbui Media, Gusserane, Co. Wexford

Printing: Swiftprint Solutions Ltd.
Rathnew, Co. Wicklow.


Distribution: Gill Group,
Hume Avenue, Park West, Dublin 12.
Tel +353 (1)500 9500


ISBN: 978-0-9573162-7-0

To Nelly and Michael Joyce
who built a warm nest and
scattered magic and wonder
over their seven wonderful
daughters and four sons.

# Acknowledgements

Many, many thanks to the wonderful people who inspired me and guided me in the writing of this book.

Thank you to all my family and my great friends and especially to:

My advisor Shirley Connolly for planting the seed in 2012 and for scribbling on a sheet of paper several times, "a book, a book, please write your book". "What book?" I asked. She said mysteriously: "Don't come back here unless you have it written". Well here it is Shirley.

My great friend Regina Cunningham who heard that I had started the process of writing and pointed me in the direction of a publisher.

My family who surprised me by giving me a laptop a few Christmases ago when they heard that a publisher thought the bones of *A Reason to Love More* had potential.

My friend Geraldine Murphy who believed that I could write this book.

The anonymous reviewer who appraised my manuscript and wrote that I should go ahead and get it published.

My son, Daron, my daughter, Sarah, and friend, Eimear Hester who squeezed a copy of the manuscript out of locked arms and returned it to me with positive feedback by the bucketload.

My beautiful daughter and secretary, Lailah, now aged 10, who took calls and notes, who sat in on meetings and who took time out from her busy schedule to write her own book titled UP, a magical little story that may be published one day.

**– Anne Joyce**

# CONTENTS

# FOREWORD

Alzheimer's is a life-changer. From the first pale, unnoticed symptom to the inevitable conclusion, the patient and his or her family travel an unchartered road. This type of dementia can come out of the blue; only hindsight will give you the chronology of the personal descent into Alzheimer's.

When someone close to you loses their faculties and their independence, what do you do? What *can* you do?

When Nelly Joyce was diagnosed with Alzheimer's, her children set out with their mother along her lonely path to guide her with loving arms, and helped to manage her illness as best they could in difficult circumstances with frightening episodes and heart-breaking situations on all sides. Their way of coping with and, ironically, 'enjoying' their mother and each other at this time was a revelation.

A sensitively told, day-by-day account of the emotion, the challenges almost beyond human endurance and the joy that small victories can bring, gives insight that numerous technical reports can never do.

Anne Joyce in this sad, funny, uplifting and true account of the journey from the day her sisters thought that something was 'not quite right' with their mam's behaviour gives an insight that only those who have experienced Alzheimer's can understand. She offers another way to handle one of the cruellest diseases of all. Her compelling story offers hope, meaning and reward. That is the enigma.

**Helen Ashdown, editor**

> *"I was her baby, now she is mine,*
> *this little old lady of eighty-nine.*
>
> *I do for her what she did for me,*
> *when as a child I sat on her knee."*

**Rebecca Power**

# Our angel

First of all it presented itself so subtly and quietly, just like me Mam's character. I was in total denial and disbelief for a while as each time I went to see her in the early stage she appeared to be her old self. My sisters were telling a different story. They found Mam was not exactly herself. She was forgetting to turn off the gas cooker. She was overloading the fuel cooker. She was forgetting to take a shower, repeating herself, cremating the homemade brown bread and driving the car like a bat out of hell.

My mother Ellen Joyce was a gift, an inspiration, a lady who never judged people, filled with simplicity, kindness, blessed, topped to the brim with soul, wisdom and no nonsense. She had absolutely no desire for materialism.

My forever memory of Mam is a lady of few words, a warm kitchen, home cooking, card games, quietness, and prayer. Her few words whenever spoken were as simple as: "People in glass houses should never throw stones" or "There but for the grace of God go I". There was never room in her serene demeanour for either complaint, gossip or a tongue lashing. She did not judge or give advice. Somewhere deep inside her soul she knew words were unnecessary and that all would be well no matter what landed on her doorstep. She was our very own angel.

Mam was self-educated. She was well-read and knew the importance of roots, self-respect, responsibility and endurance with lightness. Many times I went home with stuff that I thought would rattle her but all I ever encountered was a loving tear and a knowing smile.

It makes me wonder about the concept of reincarnation – had Mam been around the block a few times? Is this the reason why some people stress over not having the sheets turned back while others wouldn't lose a night's sleep if a freight train derailed taking the gable end clean off their house. Don't get me wrong. Mam was not disconnected in any way; she simply had the ability to see around things and had a continuous light at the end of her tunnel. Her beautiful heart and spirit did not appear to carry unnecessary stress and negativity into her own world. She'd regularly say: "Don't make a mountain out of a molehill".

When Alzheimer's eventually took hold there were still times in the day where Mam floated back into the real world and seemed perfectly normal. But with its cunning it began to gather momentum. It started to become very real and with unshakeable determination began to dig deeper and deeper into her being. It became clear that Alzheimer's was gradually going to steal our Mam away and leave a completely different version of her in its wake.

I scrambled at times on my hands and knees with readjustment and acceptance until eventually, a beautiful new way of loving bloomed.

Irish poet and author John O'Donohue puts it like this: 'Suffering can call us forward into a new rhythm of belonging which will be flexible and free enough to embrace our growth'.

# The Lion King

In my secret world I called my Da the Lion King on the light days when we were talking. He was the anchor of our big ship. He was the boss, the foundation, the captain. I told him many, many times he was blessed to have met Mam as she saw the wonder underneath his hard intolerant exterior. There was no doubt that Da's awkwardness and fire did not consume her. He was the storm and she was the calm. He demanded attention and respect not so much verbally – you just smelt it a mile away, knowing instinctively whose house you were in. He had pride and honesty written all over him.

God knows at times he was lacking in the patience and affection department. He also suffered periodically from anxiety. I can only say this now, looking back. Just like me, he found confidence and the ease of life nicely packaged in a dark bottle labelled Guinness and a shot of the rare stuff. He was not an alcoholic thank goodness. Me Mam handed him back a few pound on a Friday night out of his wages and depending on the work shift, he might just get cleaned up in his Sunday best and cycle to the local three miles away. When he was in good order he would bring ice-cream home for us children. He was our superhero for a while.

Years later when we had started to leave the nest and the

burden of supporting a large family eased, he took a few too many at times. I remember him falling off the bike into the ditch after a right old session and doing a smashing job on his nose. Man, it was some sight. It seemed like it took years for the swelling to go down. Nobody mentioned the state of his nose or suggested a doctor; it would heal as he soaked up bog water through his feet. Da swore by a cup of black tea, while soaking his feet in a bog hole after saving turf. Maybe he was right. He certainly had good health into his late seventies. He then was put on some medication for his heart. But he only administered the dose when he felt it necessary and certainly not as prescribed. You see, bless him, like me Mam, he also had a bit of wisdom hidden away in his back pocket.

But Da did well despite his very own anxiety gene. I only learned after he passed away that his mother had died giving birth to her youngest child when Da was only six years of age. The nurturer of the Joyce family was whipped away before her time. Maybe this contributed to Da's feeling of unease in dealing with the trials of engaging with his very own eleven children. The remaining family then had to work the land with a baby in tow afraid of the authorities as in those days men weren't seen to be competent child carers. All it would have taken was one nosy parker to put the spanner in the works and Grandad Joyce may have lost his little chicks to the cruelty man.

I tried my living best to keep in Da's good books. But he came from an era of mending fences by accepting your lot in life. His offspring were of a different era. The mould was about to be broken whether he liked it or not. Out of seven daughters we presented four divorces. Of course the lads were all saints marrying wonderful women who could help master their storms with the same quantity of patience and wisdom as me Mam.

God forbid, while on my father's watch one certainly did not get pregnant outside of marriage. Nor did you attempt to leave a spouse or you had a definite strike against you for a term or two, until eventually something softened within him. Maybe Mam's ability to accept all our little and big hurdles, just like she accepted the seasons, saved us from total ridicule.

Ah, this relationship with my father was oftentimes fraught with angst. I remember the ease I felt after he passed away knowing that our final battle of wills was well and truly put to rest. Don't get me wrong. He probably would have felt the same had I popped my clogs first. We both had unrealistic expectations of each other given our rearing and psychological warfare.

Unfortunately for me poor Da, I took the road less travelled and sought out professional help for my anxiety in my late twenties, only to be sent to his door to discuss all my trials. I feel now it was a ridiculous thing to do. This poor man had not a clue what to do with me. He was not equipped to deal with my anxiety, not to mind his own. Was I expecting this great big man to flip over, hug me and take my cares away when he did not know what the word emotion meant? Emotion was from a foreign land.

The suggestion to build a different type of relationship with my father was the rock I would perish on. It was as good as throwing me to the wolves. Da had neither basis nor education on how to support us in an emotional way. I had no idea what I was looking for. Each so called "bonding" session ended with him screaming while shaking so much that the foundations of the house were under threat, as I cradled my head in my hands in case it would explode with tension.

I remember one such encounter telling him I was divorcing my husband of six years. I left the house a cracked nut with a black migraine, feeling that I had let him down terribly. Two weeks after that bonding session, he left a wooden box filled with potatoes and onions on the landing of my new home, turned on his heels and as he walked away he said, "You'll be alright".

I am crying as I am writing this now as I still feel for him. Like so many others of his generation, he did absolutely brilliantly keeping his head above water, putting food on the table and fuel in the fire for over fifty years.

Summed up, my father was an old style gent, a warrior, a great provider and a wonderful card player. He knew when to take chances adding a bit of mischief and mystery to the game that only he could get away with. Nobody would ever dare pull up the Lion King. He had honour galore, he was proud as punch and he adored his daughters and sons-in-law. Even when he was out cold with us he still held a place in his heart for them. He was a good neighbour, a good son-in-law, a great employee, and he had within him great character. At times he could make a cat laugh.

He was straight up. He did not run with the hare and hunt with the hound. He abhorred dishonesty. He tried his best with what his background had given him and his positives outweighed the grey cloud of stubbornness, his tunnel vision and his dreaded anxiety.

Yes, it's so true. To understand is to pardon. Da was certainly an important thread in our tapestry and I was shocked to find myself on my knees with grief when he passed away. I suddenly was left with the realisation that I was cut from the same cloth and that behind my own stubbornness and anxiety was laid a well-worn blanket of love for this man.

Da was blessed in more ways than one. First of all to take Mam's hand in marriage and then to leave this world in his eighties suddenly without warning or prolonged discomfort. He did not have to face the wait and discomfort of a long, slow exit.

The day before he was due to return from hospital after tests, he had a massive heart attack. He went on his merry way with not so much as a farewell leaving behind him an unfillable void. No more commentary on the quality of his turf or the growth of his tomatoes or potatoes. No more snoring in the middle of the day or knocking on the kitchen door as he passed. Little did we know that the loss of my Da was going to be so apparent and in his place came a tangible vacant atmosphere in our cottage on the hill.

# Da

Moving to Offaly was a chance that Mike took,
and who would believe in his stroke of good luck.
For a beautiful woman his eyes they did log,
she was residing in our native bog.

He worked on that bog for many long years,
day and night with his blood, sweat and tears.
His wages he used to rear eleven good childer,
who managed most times him to bewilder.

But for the cards, turf and the pint,
he wouldn't have been half the big giant.
A man we now know and remembered with love,
now that he's gone to the great pub above.

*Written by Geraldine Joyce and read to the
congregation at Da's funeral.*

# Ellen Carty Joyce

My mother Ellen Carty Joyce was born on 22nd of September 1930 in a little village called Walsh Island in the midlands of Ireland. It was a time of economic depression and it was just eight years after Ireland got independence and a decade before World War II. At the age of twenty-one, she duly married me Da, Michael Joyce "the love of her life", on the 10th of August 1952, and they eventually settled a few miles from her original home place. Without further ado, one after another, eleven children landed on her lap – seven beautiful daughters and four strong, handsome sons.

I want to give you a little glimpse into Mam's world. Reading many true stories of Ireland back in those days I know we were blessed, for the biggest part of our world was a safe refuge. We were washed, dressed, kept warm and well fed. Mam provided a little haven for eleven children and her man.

She was not just good at it. She was much more – she was just amazing, wonderful. She had the ability to keep the wolf from the door, getting up early each morning for over fifty years to start the day by shaking down the fire. The sound of the house coming alive in the morning is still with me. There were no dishwashers, washing machines, or Hoovers. In the first few years of married life the water came from a community pump in the next field so she carried water in buckets day after day. She was happy with her lot and felt blessed that me Da had a job, a bike and there was enough of a wage to keep us all watered, fed and out the door, as the wise used say in those days.

Mam did not care what the neighbours had. She had no desire to have more and when she did have extra at the end of her life, she gave the money away. I remember some members of our family telling me a story about Da's brother coming to our house when we were all grown up and in jobs, offering Da his share in the family farm in Galway. My Da sent him away with the paperwork intact, saying that it was not necessary to divide the land as he already had a comfortable living.

This is who they were. They had no need for flash cars or clothes or material possessions. They were happy to keep it simple and they knew when they had enough.

If I could bottle the feeling in Mam's kitchen and sell it I would be worth a fortune. She must have been the cleverest woman I have ever known because we did not need to question anything. There was always enough. She could do what needed doing without fuss or being stressed and she managed to do it mostly by herself. Even when we needed a doctor she put us on the back of her bike and cycled the seven or eight miles into town never complaining.

She found a cure for everything, chicken pox, measles, the jaundice, flus and colds and there was always more than one poorly at a time. She created Christmas out of nothing. She sewed, darned, wallpapered, painted, and in the early days kept a garden and a few pigs and hens for eggs. She produced these great dinners, breads, puddings and apple tarts. She had the patience of a saint answering our questions and keeping the house quiet when me Da returned from work.

No matter what landed on her lap as we grew into adults she remained calm, never once a word of disappointment, judgement, or anger. Her answer to everything was a prayer and a cup of tea. Bet you think I am making this up but it is true. She was presented with so many challenges and life experiences but miraculously managed to remain dignified, calm and supportive.

I remember going home at forty to tell both my parents that I was having a baby out of wedlock. Mam's immediate response was a blessing. She was so graciously accepting it was easy to go to her. Little did she know that baby, Lailah, was to become her playmate during the Alzheimer's years. So she was right again – her latest grandchild was indeed a blessing.

I can tell you me Da's reaction was the exact opposite. He knew well before any announcement of a shiny new addition to his flock. He did not talk to me for almost two years. Mam and he were like chalk and cheese but she thought the world of Da regardless. She knew it was only a matter of time. So what if it took a few years; she never once spoke of his dismissal of me. She allowed him be. He was the one who ran away from problems. Da did not want to know and thankfully she was able to take them gently into her heart and nurture them until the ripples in the pond stilled. A clever lady. I remember clearly as a child wanting to hide under her apron. The only place I ever felt safe was in that kitchen and I thank goodness that I had a chance to make my kitchen a little haven for her at times in her last few years.

As children, we walked to Mass every Sunday, hail, rain or snow, shoes a shining and hair neatly tied back in ribbons. We sat quietly and respectfully like little lambs. Her calmness had this effect on us. She had a little valley running down the centre of her left thumb nail and she ran her other thumb nail down that valley repeatedly unknown to herself while she sat among us praying for patience. It was her little habit. Funny the things you remember.

She was devoted to the Catholic Church but she was never drawn into a discussion on religion. She didn't preach it but as we got older she insisted that while we were living under her roof we attend Sunday Mass. This was her support and I firmly believe it was where she found peace, comfort and patience to deal with the endless challenges of raising eleven children and keeping house. She had the ability to bless everything and everyone in a quiet manner. She was not showy and did not possess tunnel vision. Unlike my father, she could see around corners. Da could only see what he wanted to see. But together they created a balance.

Now, I am well aware that at times I can have a bit of me Da in me, his tunnel vision, stubbornness, and honesty,  with a nice handful of me Mam's care, and compassion thrown in for good measure. Alzheimer's gave me the opportunity to see these characteristics and pushed me towards maturity, maybe a "step or two"  towards real growth, wisdom and understanding.

It crucified all of us when Alzheimer's presented itself. Mam was gradually to face depression and discontentment and this in our eyes was unacceptable as she never complained and was so accommodating. It was hard to accept that Mam had to experience this sentence. But we will reach for the little flickers of hope and light.

# The penny drops

The awful sad feeling I had the day I realised that the opportunity had passed to know my mother on a deeper level haunts me. I had always had this curiosity about how she ticked, how she could restrain herself from exploding when one of us eleven presented her with some more bullshit. How was she so accepting? Was she a slow reactor? What I mean is, when she heard disturbing news, did she not get the impact until it had naturally resolved itself. Or did she just sit quietly on the fence and pray for the best of each situation afraid to give her opinion for fear of saying the wrong thing.

Funny thing is I never felt any lingering discomfort in her. She was not uptight and she seemed to move gently like a leaf floating down stream around obstacles rather than trying to get through them, avoiding carrying extra baggage. There is also the case of Mam having just about as much as she could handle to keep home for eleven children and a husband. I remember her saying when we were in school, "Don't come home here asking questions, ask the teacher. That's what they're there for".

I guess there was a little bit of me thinking after Da died that at last we have her all to ourselves, to explore, to get under her skin and find out who she really was. But

Alzheimer's came along and robbed me of this opportunity. Or maybe it saved her from the interrogation.

Now I felt I would never know if she was naturally a wise soul, handing each dilemma into God's care, believing that her prayers would be answered. She came from an era of "least said, soonest mended". Maybe her mentors, her own mother, her best friend, Poll, her sisters or someone else in her youth had imprinted these wise sayings on her soul. Or maybe it was the Catholic Church with its doctrine of "he who casts the first stone", stay off the judgment pedestal. Or maybe it was just good old St. Theresa and her wisdom of "This too shall pass." Who knows where me Mam's calm exterior came from. We certainly were never going to get to the bottom of it now.

Mam was not dramatic. She took each day and did her best always starting with prayer and ending in thanksgiving. I guess we could all take a lesson from that.

For me, because she was not giving of opinion, I have found it difficult to be confident in my own views. I have been afraid at times to speak up where it may have been necessary and shut up where it may have been better to stay quiet. Maybe just like her, I should patiently watch for the resolution, to be more considerate and kind and master the art of acceptance.

I live in hope that one day I will say something profound and get a real kick out of moving off the fence for a second or two and feel me Mam's wings gathering momentum.

# Forgetting

**M**am was forgetting what she was doing. She was forgetting during a task, such as leaving the gas cooker on after lifting a saucepan. She was forgetting to take showers. She was becoming confused while dressing. She was forgetting the time of day, date, month, and year. Knowing that Mam was normally the queen of calm and completed each task without distraction before moving on to the next, it was easy to tell there was something wrong.

According to documented research there are seven definitive stages of Alzheimer's and many subtle stages within these steps. At the time of our first awakening, someone in our family gave us an information sheet which outlined our future journey with Mam. When I read the sheet at the beginning it was easy to pick out where Mam stood on the timeline. According to these notes, it was becoming very clear that there was considerably more than old age on the horizon.

Reading through the stages from one to four clarified that Mam was definitely showing signs of Alzheimer's. And by the time I read through to the very end, I was in absolute shock at what could follow if you were unfortunate enough to reach the latter part of stage seven – a possible breakdown of the mind, senses, and bodily functions. I immediately began to pray that Mam would never reach that point.

A few short days after Da's sudden death, she appeared to retreat or had we missed something way before then, as the focus at that time was on *his* wellbeing? Seeming to be her usual self, considering she had already survived bowel cancer and was given a possible five years more, I cannot say the exact duration from the beginning stages of her experience with Alzheimer's. But I would place my bets on those long four years and Da's sudden death a possible instigator. The fact that after this point she was also told to give up cigarettes before further assessment may have set her back also. There is a belief that cigarettes can have a calming effect and, whatever damage they may have caused, the negative side of this habit had been well and truly done at this stage. The withdrawal may have affected her equilibrium.

I guess the amount of time one moves through each stage is individual and unique depending on other health issues, adequate care and the call of nature. The following is just my interpretation. It's not set in stone. At times I have had a job drawing this information from my memory.

I am giving the reader a little glimpse of the whole story before telling of Mam's daily struggles and challenges. I have an impatient type of personality and I have an itch to know what happened and how it was addressed in the here and now. It's a bit like wanting to ride a bike before you have fallen off a hundred times.

The experts tell us that occasionally forgetting why you came into a room or what you planned to say, like forgetting names or appointments now and again, constitutes normal age-related forgetfulness.

Right now at fifty years of age, I am forgetting names and what I had planned to say. So I guess I must be normal to some degree, at least some of the time. I know some of my family will laugh at this one but I will turn a humorous blind eye and move forward. If there were changes in Mam at this stage it wasn't noticed because she was living on her own, keeping up with her card playing, church going, visiting and her weekly bingo excursion. She naturally spoke little and therefore it would be hard to tell if she was forgetting to communicate to any degree.

# The cat is out of the bag

With repeated queries, inability to organise and concentration deficits, she now has mild cognitive impairment. I guess this is where it all began. At stage three there was no doubt that the cat was out of the bag and my mother's life deteriorated. There was a little more going on than growing old.

I remember Mam before nursing home care getting confused while dressing and forgetting to wash or take a shower. At night time not long after retiring she would wake, get up, and prepare for the day in the middle of the night. She could be found sitting at the kitchen table with her tea, eggs, and toast and flicking through her prayer book at two or three in the morning, oblivious to the time. Back then we tried to stay overnight with her for security reasons but she had no interest in our company. She was becoming a stranger and she was sure glad to see the back of us when we left the following morning.

Mam had to be reminded of appointments constantly and told to ring a friend to organise her card playing or social outings in the evening time. Her concentration had started to wither. Once a great card player for over thirty five years, she started to make silly mistakes and seemed to be smug while cheating, dismissing correction with a bold smile. This was unlike her normally polite, honest character; if she took a step over any line, an automatic sorry would be assured. A member of her team told me that Mam had also started eating the goodies during the tea breaks as if they were going out of fashion. While driving at this stage she appeared to be away with the fairies. Neither one of us nor her card-playing buddies wished to travel with her while she was behind the wheel and by the luck of God she didn't cause an accident involving others.

# Forgetting more …

orgetting the days of the week and where you are going, getting lost in your own neighbourhood, less emotional response, withdrawal, decreased ability to prepare meals or manage finances. This is stage four.

Mam was by nature a very quiet lady. Therefore it took longer to see that she was slowly withdrawing. But I do remember at this stage before Alzheimer's crossed our minds, my brother Mike saying on occasion that Mam was responding less and less and making no attempt to converse. It felt like she wanted to be left alone. After many scrapes and near misses, Mam did eventually lose her way in the car and had an accident while returning home on a dark winter's night from card playing. I remember going into her kitchen the next day to be met by a bold grin as if her heart had been recharged and her spirit had re-emerged. But it was clear also that there was no shock element. It was as if she was unaware of her actions.

Geraldine said that when she collected Mam from the hospital that night she was unfazed after driving the car down a steep embankment in pitch darkness, many miles from her intended destination. When asked what she was doing at the time she said, "Saying my prayers". The angels must have been by her side while she scrambled back to safety.

Her only injuries were mild scratches. I know her card-playing buddies were as relieved as we were that her car had to be towed to the scrap yard. Her days of driving had come to a close.

Around the same time, Mam lost interest in cooking and started to order sandwiches from the local shop. Most of the time she didn't eat the sandwiches.

To try and keep Mam occupied and interested in something, my sister insisted that she continue the tradition of baking brown bread to satisfy her grandchildren. It wasn't long before the bread started to be cremated. But this didn't bother her. It was still wrapped up neatly and given to my sister for her tea. We got such a laugh out of this at the time. I remember going into Mam's kitchen one day to find a line of bread on the counter. Some of the cakes were black as coal and the gas cooker was still blazing. It was not unusual to find the cooker turned on with no flame alight. She'd made an attempt to boil water for tea, forgot what she was doing, and the house filled with gas fumes. At this stage my brothers cut the gas line to the cooker and pretended that the cooker was unfixable and installed an electric hob.

Then I'm afraid, to put the tin hat on it, one winter's evening Mam climbed up on a delicate little table to close the bedroom curtains, tumbled backwards and broke her wrist and hip. I think she was giddy from the painkillers she was taking at the time. What she was taking them for, we still don't know.

Mam was not used to taking drugs. She was no climber but out of the blue yonder she got a sense of adventure and made a precarious decision which resulted in a trip to the hospital and from there into nursing home care to convalesce. Maybe it was God's helping hand in making the decision of care with Alzheimer's easier for us.

# It's now moderate

The Alzheimer's patient can often become angry and suspicious. They need a care-giver to prepare adequate food and help them dress as some people begin to wear the same clothes every day and choose inappropriate clothing. They also may show poor judgement and give away large sums of money.

At the beginning of stage five, Mam became angry and suspicious. It was understandable considering she had no awareness of her condition and thought we were all trying to trick her. The misplaced purse, glasses and Rosary beads along with many other items were a great big bone of contention for some time. Although the nurse explained that payment was not necessary, Mam tried without success to give staff members money for assisting her. She insisted that one of us search for her purse while she played cards or bingo in the dayroom.

I remember around this time Mam was found in her bedroom happily colouring her toe nails with black permanent marker.

At the end of stage five, she began to mess with her food. She would shake the salt seller for Ireland and overload her tea with sugar. These items then had to be removed from her table.

I remember one day being afraid that Mam would lash out at another resident who had dementia, while she watched his moves intently with a face of thunder as he leaned forward. I imagine she thought he was going to take her food. During this phase it was common for Mam to brazenly take food off Lailah's plate. I can still remember Lailah's little voice saying, "Nanny is eating my food again".

As Mam became more troubled, she lost interest in everything. Impatience and irritation then gradually set in with six-year old Lailah. Out of the blue on several occasions I caught her wildly raising a hand while shouting at her to go away. This was in contradiction to Mam's normal calm behaviour. Up to this point they had been happy in each other's company and would happily sit together while playing games or reading.

Around the end of stage five, when Lailah produced playing cards, Mam threw them across the table and sat staring into space. Only months before this, Mam asked if she could take 'the young one' back to the nursing home with her for company.

# It's moderate to severe

Toilet paper, pads and newspapers were stuffed everywhere. They were even under Mam's cardigan. The supplies had been removed from the shower room because on occasion the toilet was filled to the brim with toilet paper or other such items.

Most mothers will tell a similar story of finding themselves in the same predicament while going through the toddler stage of child rearing. Mam now needed to wear incontinence pads as her brain was not sending her the message to use the toilet. When assisted she was liable to get confused and would neither lead nor drive.

Her attention span was fading rapidly. I would settle down to do something with her only to find there was absolutely no engagement or interest. Losing interest in food was the final straw as that had been the only comfort she had left. Now she was having to be spoon-fed and encouraged constantly to take sips of liquid. Lack of liquid caused serious bouts of dehydration, hallucinations and long stretches of emotional upheaval. It was a common occurrence to find Mam in bits, weeping, filled with hopelessness, despair and sadness. At the end of stage six we had to stop taking Mam outside the nursing home as her mobility had started to become an issue.

According to the manual, "The Alzheimer's patient at this stage will need assistance dressing and toileting. They may put toilet tissue in the wrong place, forget to flush and become incontinent".

# It's stage seven

The manual continued: "Speech becomes more limited. They lose the ability to sit up without support and the ability to walk independently. At the end of this stage the patient may develop rigidity and joint deformities which make movement impossible without pain."

It had become impossible for Mam to sit upright now. Sadly, she was starting to spend her days slumped over in uncomfortable positions in the dayroom. She was now speechless, expressionless and motionless. She eventually ended up around the clock in her bedroom refusing food and drinks.

Thankfully she could still be moved slowly and gently for bed changes and bathing without discomfort or, my greatest fear, the use of a "hoist". It was impossible to administer enough liquid, leaving her even more dehydrated and becoming more lifeless, drifting in and out of sleep states. When she was awake, she had no expression. There was that look of bewilderment of "nobody is at home".

Mam went from stage five to stage seven in approximately two years. Thank goodness she did not reach the stage where the limbs seize up, causing deformities and rigidity.

We were blessed she was a resident in a modern, up-to-date facility and had the cosiness of a wonderful air mattress which was constantly readjusted for comfort and movement. There were no bed sores to contend with. Yes, my prayers were answered.

# Hindsight

Looking back now the day after we got the news that Da had died suddenly, I felt a shift in Mam. I remember she seemed to be in no man's land. She was lost. I could not put words on it. Maybe she was just in shock. You might say well isn't it obvious? It's grief. But it was much more than that. The mother I knew was nowhere to be found. Her direction and her purpose for living had vanished. She wasn't ready to let him go.

In her mind, Da was back on his feet in the hospital, in good form and she was prepared for his return to the nest. Alas this was not to be. Instead of a calm environment, her home was suddenly filled with busyness. We were all pulling the house together for the stream of visitors that was to come to pay their respects. Mam had said her morning prayers and seemed lost amongst all of us. It was clear she did not want to entertain. Maybe she needed space to grieve in peace and clear her head. It is much easier to take action when someone outside the family dies. Daily routine is changed for a short period of time. But Mam's life was changed forever.

Da was gone. No more cup and saucer placed on the table before bed, no more porridge soaking through the night on the edge of our fuel cooker. No more interpretation of the news, the soaps, or the weather forecast.

After retirement, Da had his own little retreat in the sitting room where he watched TV. Mam had her own TV in the kitchen. Da gave a running commentary on world events or local news several times a day. Even if they didn't talk, wasn't he her life partner? They could sit in silence in their separate caves. He was company – a life to share the day, a reason to get up in the morning and go to the village and get the newspaper. It was the end of fifty three years of together-ness. Her little cottage was going to be very quiet.

Mam obviously loved me Da enormously as she "never" said one word against him. There was very little struggle in their relationship. It was the euphony of one-sided uncon-ditional love. She was a dream wife and at times he was moody, temperamental, and stubborn. Mam had the ability to make his life so very pleasant; she was the calm in the storm, the gentleness in the background.

When we were children if Da was in bad form, she was able to keep the house calm and would take his meals to his room where he would take refuge until his humour changed. The flip side of this is that he was her strength, her motivator and she needed him as much as he needed her. They were good together and good for each other.

Someone once told me that there are three important things to keep the spirit alive: someone to love, something to do and something to look forward to. Well, for Mam on several levels, life changed in one fell swoop. First of all she lost her great love – Da. Then she lost her way coming home from playing cards one night and drove the car off the road which led to her losing her independence. We had noticed she had begun to drive erratically, taking chances, speeding and driving on the wrong side of the road. This was the opportunity to try and persuade her to stop driving. This double whammy interfered with her "get up and go" and her independence. Her interest in everything began to dissipate. It took the shine off excursions leaving her with nothing to look forward to. Or maybe it was nothing to do with all of the above. Maybe it was just Alzheimer's lurking in the background ready to snatch another victim at a low ebb.

Some believe that Alzheimer's may be a way to retreat when one has no will to live after the loss of a life or independence. They call it the "long goodbye". It is not the same when you have to depend on others. It is much sweeter to put the key in the ignition and zoom along on your own merry way especially when you live in the countryside.

I remember Mam used to take the newspaper to her friend Poll each morning for something to do after Da passed. When the car was gone she tried to get one of us to make that delivery. We explained to her that Poll had her own paper and it was not necessary. But Mam would hand it over with a smile each day as we left the house. In the end to pacify her, we just graciously accepted it which led her to believe we would carry out this message.

At this stage it was evident that Mam's short-term memory and her ability to focus properly was diminishing. Hindsight is a great thing. I bet she did not even read the newspaper herself but she could not make a decision to discontinue another little habit or routine which held her day together.

# The long goodbye

**M**y sister, Perry, believes that there is a perfect reason for everything and if you are lucky enough to view the world through rose-tinted glasses, Alzheimer's must eventually reveal some positive aspects or lessons even if it is just a leg up the perseverance ladder while dragging a reluctant sliver of hope from the depths of our own souls.

Don't get me wrong. Alzheimer's in itself is a miserable condition with no good intention but to strip away all joy and clear the house leaving an empty shell. The only hope any patient has in the beginning is to pray that their number may be called sooner rather than later.

My thoughts, feelings and experiences of Mam during the Alzheimer's years are contained in little flickers of memories from old and some of the influences of my rearing in Mam's warm kitchen. It may seem I was on my own during this time because I am reluctant to include the word "we" too often. I do not want you to think for one moment that my family and friends agree at all times with my interpretation of this journey. As I know only too well we each view the world and Alzheimer's through many different lens. This undertaking was divided among many. If we were to agree on any one member of our family getting top score for going to the nursing home many times day after day, it would be my sister Geraldine. I cannot take any more credit than the rest. The only difference is that I had a desire to document my relationship with Alzheimer's and all it entailed. It may or may not resonate with the same strength for other members of my family or the world in general.

The wonderful thing is that we had an army of support. My siblings and in-laws, neighbours, Mam's relations and friends fell into a natural rhythm of care. I doubt if there was a day that Mam went without visitors unless the nursing home was on lock-up to prevent a virus spreading. Even then we always had my younger sister Sarah who can turn a blind eye to almost all restrictions. No bug would halt her gallop.

We also had the support of our very own angels, sister-in-law Mary G, the nursing home medical staff, wonderful care workers and many other families on the corridors of the nursing home living through similar experiences. One day they might find their loved one in a peaceful state and the next despair, wanting to die before every faculty was worn to a thread. Each visitor and carer had one heartfelt intention to be Mam's bridge in her thought pattern, to encourage her to make the next steps in each task before her senses diminished completely and the darkness truly descended, to fill the isolation within this dismal condition. They were an unending stream of help.

I entered into this on my feet and I joyfully skipped through it on my sunny days. There were days when I shamefully dragged my heels. There were many days when I crawled on my hands and knees out to the car park after a visit, trying to hold back an avalanche of obscene words or tears. On those dark miserable days I can tell you that Alzheimer's had a lot to answer for. My language never recovered as I am now known to use swearwords with fire, nearly as bad as me Da years ago when he was on a rampage. Mam was a different kettle of fish. If you were to put a gun to her head she would not utter even the simplest of swear words. Her best attempt was "Oh, Sugar" with gusto if she forgot something or if it started to rain while the washing was flapping on the line.

Now that Mam is gone and I can look back, it is clear to see that Alzheimer's gave us the opportunity to love her unconditionally and each other more than one could think possible and to show our appreciation for her through unwavering attention, the misery and the laughter.

Mam got the chance to show many hidden sides of herself that would certainly not have been revealed had Alzheimer's not come to her door. She got to express disappointment, grief, love and laughter, to be playful, to act crazily, to express her anger and to be bluntly honest like a child with no reservations. She got to down tools and give up, throw her hands up in the air and say 'this is ridiculous', just like Da when he was frustrated.

It was fascinating to see other parts of her personality emerge through Alzheimer's. You know what they say: 'Watch out for the quiet ones'. Mam had high standards but during this time she got to cheat at cards. She would rob the top card without remorse. It was amusing to see her being playful and childlike. I remember while growing up wondering why she ever went to Confession unless, inwardly, she was planning to slaughter us all. Outwardly, she was an absolute saint.

Another positive in acceptance of Mam's condition is that it gave us the opportunity to come together as a family. It drew out the best in us and I found within myself strength and perseverance that I would have otherwise denied I had. I cannot count the number of times I was moved to tears as I watched other family members demonstrate incomparable love and devotion to Mam, and their sadness and broken hearts while they experienced her descent into the ugliness of this condition.

She was surrounded by many helping hands and loving hearts. You would have to be blind to miss the many blessings our family was to meet as time moved us further along the path. We crashed together; we cried rivers of tears together; we got frustrated and angry together but we also had many laughs and wonderful encounters mingled throughout the struggles and we were truly blessed to have each other to share the joy and the pain.

My brother, Fergus, started cooking Sunday dinners so that we could all be together in the one location for Mam once she started living in the nursing home. These dinners are continuing today. If Mam had ended her time naturally these get-togethers would not have happened. My sister, Perry, said that maybe Alzheimer's had some hidden gifts to prepare us for life without Mam and because of her long goodbye, our glass remained half full.

# A note of caution

Someone told me the story of a mother and daughter driving through a busy town and approaching a junction. The daughter is shocked as her mother shoots through a red light, but as they are both safe says nothing to avoid argument. Moments later her mother drives through a second set of red traffic lights. The daughter automatically recoils with horror: "Mam do you realise we have just driven through two sets of red lights?" Her mother responds with great surprise, "Why, my dear, there were no lights."

I gave a note to Mam sometime after she had had the car accident. Before this point she had terrified myself and others by driving on the wrong side of the road, shooting out of slip roads without caution and without doubt, judging by the state of the car, had driven off her path several times. Thank God the only damage done was to the car.

Although she did give me a smile after reading the note, it was inevitable that she would struggle with the loss of her independence. It was an enormous setback for her at the time, but Mam never again mentioned the subject of not being allowed to drive the car . I know there are several ways to skin a cat but writing a note may be worth considering. It leaves less room for arguments and it can save on confrontation, giving the person on the receiving end time to consider the reasons or details.

On the other hand, if I had to deliver the same note to me Da it would have been wise to drop it in the letter box and run like hell. It was easy to tell by the way he brushed the last few strands across his bald patch that he wasn't jumping up and down about ageing. It was easier to approach Mam even though I knew full well she was battling with the loss of her freedom.

My letter read:

> *Mam,*
>
> *Because of your age, things are changing. I feel from my last experience in the car with you that you are not as aware as you were previously driving. In my opinion your reflexes and concentration are not up to par or at a level for safe driving. I am asking you to consider this seriously, if there was an accident and someone was killed or injured while you were driving, I would not be able to live with myself, had I not said this to you.*
>
> *You are eighty years of age; it is inevitable that your thought patterns, awareness and ability to make quick and clear decisions on the road are not acceptable. You must now consider that you are slowing down and although this is hard you must ask yourself is your independence worth the risk of a possible lost life. Losing you would be our loss but to put others at risk would be unforgivable.*
>
> *I had to ask myself the same question for a different reason a few years ago. Was my independence worth*

*me going into more debt because at the time I couldn't afford to keep a car on the road? I missed my independence; pain in the ass as it was at the time, we all must stop now and again and make responsible decisions.*

*It is your turn to sit back and let your family take you wherever you might want to go and accept there is another way.*

*Anne*

# The hardest thing

Perhaps your eyes need to be washed by tears now and again to give you a clearer view. That's a quotation from somewhere. In the beginning, Mam prayed to die. She tried to get strangers to take her home and she made several attempts to leave the nursing home on her own. In her eyes, any open door or escape route was a blessing. I guess she felt like a prisoner wrongly committed. Who could blame her? A nursing home setting is really an extension of a hospital stay and no one in their right mind would willingly spend any more time than necessary in either establishment.

I bet even health farms lose their appeal eventually. Most of us humans long for our own homes and own beds, good or bad, at the end of each day. Mam's anxiety, depression, confusion and inability to cope therefore was understandable. Some of the able-bodied residents used to watch out for her. I remember one beautiful little lady telling me it broke her heart to see Mam standing alone with her red hat and coat on at the glass exit doors looking out longing for one of us to appear.

It reminds me of a story a friend of mine told about visiting her mother in a nursing home in Dublin. In the reception area, a woman sat every single day with her coat, hat and wheelie bag. She was there from early morning to close of day patiently waiting. When the bell rang for lunch she duly stood up and walked to the dining area. When finished she returned like clockwork to the reception area once again and took a seat only to wait until the next bell would sound. Nobody ever came. She may not have had a relative still living on this earth.

Settling your mother in to the nursing home is a bit like walking your child to the school gates for the first time. The child is wrapped firmly around your legs like superglue with a sinking feeling of being abandoned. You know you must walk away because it is the right thing to do. It's not easy. I remember this clearly with my daughter, Sarah. We all know it is a necessary next step but this knowingness will not take away their feeling of anxiety. Hard to believe that Sarah is now the queen of travel. Any more than five minutes in her homeland and she gets itchy feet. While I am writing, she is exploring Australia.

One afternoon in the early stages of nursing home care, I found Mam sitting alone on her bed waiting in an apparent sea of sadness. On occasion in the early stages she would flip right back to absolute clarity and would be in a perfect state of mind. Her hip and hand had mended sufficiently. She was ready physically to return home, but was oblivious to the fact that she now had a new companion lurking in the background. She looked at me in her normal expectant way and asked me to take her home. There were no signs of Alzheimer's at that moment and probably for some hours before. This left me in a quandary as it did repeatedly in the beginning – it had inexplicably disappeared.

I knew I had no choice but to support nursing home care but I was still torn between wanting to save Mam from the feeling of being abandoned and not knowing how desperate the Alzheimer's was going to get. I felt I had no right even considering saving her this discomfort when there was a possibility that somewhere down the road in the not too distant future, both of us might need saving. I was well aware that it would take many hands and hearts to walk alongside this condition in the later stages.

Of course I couldn't tell her she was slowly losing her mind. So I tried to explain that she was on strong medication for an illness, as before Mam broke her wrist and hip she had been seeing a specialist for bowel-related cancer. I tried my best to be convincing, telling her gently the attention of the professionals at night time to administer a concoction of drugs was crucial in order to help her sleep and remain pain free. Under no circumstances would a family member be allowed to assist.

She told me that this was a ridiculous explanation and demanded to know what we were trying to do to her, leaving her in this place.

Jesus, my heart was torn to shreds. All I wanted was for the ground to open up and swallow us both. I knew deep down this was just the tip of the iceberg. She looked frustrated and disappointed. I also knew she could see through me and that there was much more to the story. Mam spent all her life reading, doing crosswords, playing cards and scrabble. If she had this ability left it would have made the initial transition easier. The boredom and loneliness was crippling her and already it was clear that her spirit was about to dwindle right before my eyes.

This was the very first day I crawled out of the nursing home with a heavy heart and feeling like a complete failure.

My beautiful mother had never asked me for anything in her life. I felt responsible for at least some of her anxiety as I left her in that room. Yes, of course I knew if the worst was to come, it would take much more than an army of care to manage. A big part of me wanted to run back, put on her coat and take her home. But I did not know what lay ahead nor was I or anyone else equipped to handle it.

I have no idea how I walked away but I do remember being blinded by tears as I drove away having to pull into the hard shoulder at the soccer pitch where I cried for her loss of belonging, her frustration and loneliness and her right to be angry as she looked at me pleading with all her might to make sense of it all.

# Go along to get along

Recently I read this following bit of wisdom somewhere, "The one thing that does not work is to try and convince the person that has Alzheimer's otherwise". This was a lesson I had to learn the hard way. But others, including my sister, Geraldine, appeared at times to have the wherewithal to go along to get along when she was confronted with a dilemma.

Shortly after Mam was admitted to the nursing home she had a relentless desire to abandon ship, escape or run away. After many failed attempts, she wore herself out dragging that Zimmer up and down the corridors. Late one afternoon Geraldine found her in a heap of discontent and confusion. The only words she could mumble repeatedly were, "I want to die". Geraldine responded promptly, "fair enough let me get you ready".

Geraldine then settled Mam into bed while asking did she want to say anything before leaving? Was she happy that she had everything done that needed doing such as her Will in order, prayers said or any final requests to make? Mam nodded in agreement then paused, asking Geraldine to get in contact with the family and let them know she was departing. My sister took up her phone and texted the whole family saying that Mam would be making her exit that evening from this world. I remember getting that text and smiling knowing that my sister would find a solution.

Up to this point a little jelly trifle was usually enough to sway Mam in a different direction. Geraldine then said to Mam, I have that done Mam and if you are ready to go, "Off with ya," Surprisingly like a little child threatening to leave home, Mam looked in Geraldine's direction and started to smile. I am not sure if she ever brought the subject up again.

I got caught several times before the penny dropped that you must 'go along to get along'. Mam was sitting at my kitchen table one miserable winter's evening. I was just about to prepare for going back to the nursing home when she announced that she wanted to go to Mass. I said, "Mam it is too late, there is no other service today, I will take you tomorrow". She was not satisfied and repeated the sentence over and over, "I want to go to Mass". Poor Mam got more and more frustrated until eventually her tone began to escalate with a noticeable hint of aggression. I again tried to explain that it was too late but she pushed her chair back, grabbed her Zimmer with force and struggled towards the front door. I was left with no choice but to grab her coat and the car keys while shouting for Lailah, then aged five, to run ahead and hold the door open.

Boy, was I frazzled. What was I going to do? I felt like a headless chicken. I knew that it was getting late and the chance of even finding a church open, not to mind a service, would be a miracle . Well, we took to the road and went to our local church first and of course there was no priest. She insisted on going to the next village. When we got there the gates were closed so I jumped out of the car opened the gates drove up to the door and said with as much enthusiasm as I could muster, "Right Mam, let's go in and say a few prayers". I could tell by her facial expression that she was beginning to realise that this was also a dead end. She immediately stalled, resisting getting out of the car. I said don't worry Mam if there is no service we will light some candles and say the Rosary. She looked like she was ready to burst into tears.

Reluctantly, Mam helped light the candles and then with half a heart wearily whispered responses to a decade of the Rosary. It was easy to tell she still had a massive bee in her bonnet and nobody but the Pope himself giving her a blessing was going to lift her spirit. I was still scrambling for some sort of solution hoping upon hope that this might just satisfy her when, just as we were about to leave the car park, she announced, "I want to go to Mass". My brain was in overdrive at this stage and I just agreed. But instead of going to the next village, I returned to the nursing home. Mam was not at all amused but when she entered the home she went straight into the toilet near reception. Then I was left wondering. What was that all about? Did she really just need to use the facilities?

It seems that Alzheimer's affects the brain in such a way that at times everything gets jumbled up and the request may be something completely different from that verbalised. One day when I was leaving Mam's bedroom she said, "Don't forget to take that firewood with you". She really meant the laundry.

I came across the following article with a bit of wisdom thrown in. After Mam's request to go to a church service, I guess the gods had to have a laugh at my expense first.

*Never say no to an Alzheimer's patient as it may take away all hope. However, they may accept delay and some uncertainty. Don't argue or ever say such things as, "This is your home now". When people with mid or late stage Alzheimer's/Dementia say, "I want to go home" they may just be saying I feel uneasy or scared. The concept of home is a mood that is soothing, familiar, and safe. Doesn't matter whether the home in the person's head is a childhood home, the home where they raised their family, or the place they live in now or all of them mingled. It is that satisfying feeling of home rather than a place.*

*Within a short period of time because of the short-term memory loss they will have forgotten what they said unless provoked and prolonged by arguing over the geography of home. Therefore, go along to get along, give a hug, be positive.*

*A little fib may be better than an argument such as the weather is too bad at the moment maybe later or the plumber has the place pulled apart at the moment and proceed to sing a song or do something to shift their attention. Remember home is where the heart is, so try to meet their emotional needs. Sit, listen, hold their hand and tell them often that you love them. This helps to reassure the person that someone cares. Remember that they might simply need some positive attention, a drink, food or simply to go to the toilet or change into more comfortable shoes or clothes.*

To think now that Mam might have just needed to go back to the nursing home while I was driving around like a lunatic looking for a church service. Ah, hindsight once again.

# An inconsiderate sentence

I was sitting in the dayroom of the nursing home with Mam who was clearly lost, staring into space. Recently people had begun asking if I thought she still recognised me. Yes, I definitely feel somewhere deep down in my gut a mother will always know her care.

A lady approaches our table and asks if I am a family member and if so, to follow her to a consultation room. In a matter of fact way after introducing herself she told me that my mother has been assessed and diagnosed with "Possible Alzheimer's Dementia". I squeeze my eyes closed as tightly as possible to stall the inevitable. Whoever said you can control your emotions. Through a thick fog of despair I hear her say, "You knew this and have been dealing with it already". I tried to collect myself but the dam was about to burst. I thought I was going to die with the pain in my chest. Through tears, I excused myself, ran to Mam's room, flung myself on the bed and sobbed uncontrollably.

While typing this story I wonder for the umpteenth time, if knowledge is key or if ignorance is actually bliss. I now knew if my mother were to live for years she would experience the later stages of the condition. But did I really want to know? Is our access to information a curse, like researching cancer when my younger sister had a breast removed at twenty-eight? Curiosity ignites a fire and leads towards the whole shebang. Although my sister survived there were times in the early stages when none of us knew and I clearly remember sitting at her imaginary funeral in my mind.

I think most people with knowledge go into shock at the point of a confirmed diagnosis. I would have preferred at the time for Mam to have had a massive heart attack and, like Da, to be spared the undignified ending some Alzheimer's patients experience. I knew right there and then the worst was to come unless she was spared it all and died suddenly.

Mam had already been praying continuously to the Lord above to take her as she spent her early days scraping her Zimmer up and down the corridors of the nursing home trying her living best to escape this "hell hole" as she described it. In her mind she was in a prison and her freedom was taken away without justification. Little did she know she was slowly losing her cognitive function and would within a short period of time begin to exist on instruction alone.

I tried to steady myself because time was ticking and I had to eventually drag myself off that bed, dry my tears and face Mam in the dayroom before collecting Lailah from school. The unfortunate thing, in my mind's eye I could see my mother's little face as I wept those tears, this beautiful lady, so graceful and calm, was given a ridiculous and inconsiderate end-of-life sentence. Sooner or later, I had no choice but to pull myself together and face Mam where I had left her, empty, staring into space in the dayroom. To my surprise her eyes met mine with a smile and I guess knowingness. She had not spoken for some days but at that moment was aware and she gave me the kindest look as if reading my despair no matter how determined I was to cover it up.

I explained to Mam that Lailah needed collecting from school. Then I turned on my heels with as much restraint as possible as I could feel a heart-breaking sob gathering in my throat again. As I walked away an emotional wreck, I heard her sweet little voice say, "God Bless Anne". I thought at that moment I might break in two. I knew without a doubt Mam was trying to tell me not to worry while all I wanted to do was scream at the gods, "Why my wonderful mother?" In that consultation room I felt the doctor had robbed the last shadow of hope I had in my heart that just maybe my Mam had depression at the shock of Da passing so suddenly and with help and the right medication she was bound to re-turn to us. But no, her mind was slowly losing its ability to function properly and she was eventually going to become a stranger, dependent and childlike.

After my meeting with the Psych Doc or Consultant, who dished out this hideous death sentence, I had a few moments to spare before collecting Lailah from school. Michael, my brother, popped in and duly became aware of my sad state. After hearing the story he advised me not to go into the nursing home to see Mam again on my own if it upset me so much and to let those able to handle damning news, do so.

Well, you can guess how shit I felt after that conversation. Talk about adding salt to my already gaping wound. I could not wait for him to leave so I could beat myself up for not receiving the news from the specialist with more grace.

Of course, after a right good battering I eventually turned the meeting with the Psych Doc on its head and realised that

I was not made of stone and had a right to feel deflated and emotional. To be honest I do not know if I ever truly accepted Alzheimer's or Dementia as a diagnosis. Who in their right mind would do so? Regardless of the fact we were blessed to have Mam in body, mind and spirit close to her eighties, the chances of this condition being kind to her were very slim. Our gentle adorable mother was slowly being replaced and her calm demeanour was being substituted with a broken spirit, disappointment, disinterest, emptiness, and if unfortunate enough, enveloped in confusion and craziness. I felt broken for her. I took comfort from the following article on listening by Dr. Susan Jackson M.D.

### A Loving Silence

*The most basic and powerful way to connect to another person is to listen. Just Listen. Perhaps the most important thing we give each other is our attention especially if it's given from the heart. When people are talking there's no need to do anything but receive them. Just take them in and listen to what they're saying. Most times, caring is even more important than understanding.*

*Most of us don't value ourselves or our love enough to know this. It has taken me a long time to believe in the power of simply saying, "I am so sorry," when someone is in pain, and meaning it. One lady told me that when she tried to tell her story people often inter-rupted to tell her that they once had something just like that happen to them. Subtly, her pain became a story about themselves. Eventually she stopped talking to most people as she was left feeling more alone.*

*We must connect by listening because when we interrupt what someone else is saying to let them know that we understand, we move the focus of attention to ourselves. When we listen, they know we care. Many people with serious illnesses talk about the relief of having someone just to listen.*

*I have learned to respond to someone crying by just listening. In the old days I used to reach for the tissues until I realized that passing a person a tissue may be another way to shut them down and to take them out of their experience of sadness and grief. Now I just listen and let them cry all they need, finding me there with them.*

*This simple thing has not been that easy to learn, as it certainly went against everything I had been taught while attending medical school. A loving silence often has far more power to heal than the most well intentioned word.*

# Let me out of here, Lord!

**M**am struggled for such a long time with being institutionalised. She had attempted to escape every other day so much so that the rubber was burnt clean off her Zimmer frame legs from dragging it up and down the corridors of the nursing home. She actually passed me in the hallway one day and did not recognise me. Blind with determination, her face as red as her winter coat and her hat shading her eyes, she must have been like a furnace with the mileage she had covered in that central heating.

We eventually agreed to have a security chip placed on the Zimmer frame but during Mam's hoarding period, she started taking the wheelie bedside table for support instead. Therefore her wandering had to be reassessed and the only other option was a security bracelet. This broke my heart not to mention hers.

I remember driving with her to my house that day. For some reason the bracelet had been fitted to her ankle, maybe in hope that Mam would not notice it or interfere with it there. It was going to take a miracle to pacify Mam while she adjusted to another unforeseen change. She was so distressed and tried her best to pull it off as we drove along. I tried every which way I could to make sense of it all by telling her it was a monitor to keep an eye on her blood levels as she had cancer. Whether Mam believed me or thought it was a load of bull I do not know, but eventually she lost interest and with it another chip off her worn-out heart.

I was truly fit to be tied and wanted to scream "Lord above! This is just ridiculous! How much more hardship does this lady have to endure?"

That night I cried myself to sleep. I felt so upset for her, the frustration of being tagged. Mam had absolutely no idea that Alzheimer's was the real traitor and that she might put herself in danger by trying to leave the nursing home. Imagine being reduced to this level of existence, to have no say in one's own well-being, no independence, robbed of the ability to make choices and to have a feeling of being caged with no control. Even though we were doing what we felt was best, this episode shook me to the core. This was "a curse" as me Da used to say. The enemy Alzheimer's was taking another shot at Mam's spirit and I once again felt shattered not being able to save her from this hell. What options had we unless someone was to sit with Mam 24/7 in case she rambled, got lost or killed on the road or caused an accident involving others.

Time and time again I remind myself that even if we had cared for Mam at home with Alzheimer's, she may have felt trapped, lost, frustrated, and angry. The chances are she might have continuously tried to leave her own home in frustration, eventually not recognising the surroundings.

My friend's uncle in New York City constantly had to get up in the middle of the night to drive his wife with Alzheimer's around the city and eventually back to their apartment in order to pacify her. She used to scream at him in terror, thinking he was a stranger.

I remember listening to the daughter of an Alzheimer's patient being interviewed on the radio. Her mother had left their home with the dog and got lost. The search party was unsuccessful. She was found a few days after her disappearance in waste land. She had died from hypothermia with her loyal companion standing guard beside her.

These stories and and others like them dragged me from despair and enabled me to appreciate the safety net and care of the nursing home.

The security bracelet was placed on Mam's wrist later that day and like everything else was forgotten by evening time. There was always a new focus around each corner as good old Alzheimer's continually had something new to offer.

Nevertheless I did wonder at times about God, this sentence and the fact that my language got way out of hand and never recovered. What was this afffliction all about and why did it come knocking on my mother's door? I still smile inwardly when people tell me that Alzheimer's patients are in a happy little world of their own. This may be true for the blessed few, but in my opinion Mam resided in anything but a contented state of mind.

When she was healthy before Alzheimer's landed in her zone, her life was a calm, simple bubble and she naturally pottered around leaning always on the side of appreciation and satisfaction. As Alzheimer's deepened, she got swallowed up by a dark cloud and unless she was well rested and had taken plenty of fluids, there was no joy, no light, and no hope in her heart or eyes.

Well, look at it this way; if suddenly you could not read, write, watch TV, listen to the radio, play cards, drive a car, wash, dress, feed or toilet independently, find peace in church, participate in activities or take a walk on the wild side, I think all bets would be off for contentment and the door would be wide open for misery.

Why, oh why, was my Mam, a gentle soul who spoke no evil and blessed every living creature in sight, subjected to this horror at the end of her journey? Ah, another little outburst from a broken-hearted daughter.

Just let me die with a skip in my step and a little bit of dignity thrown in for good measure.

# My nursing home diary

With delight, I came across our note pads from the nursing home days. It brought back memories of our journey.

As you will see, even Mam penned a few thoughts now and again along this road. These diary entries also tell a story of joy, frustration and togetherness.

These entries kept us in touch with each other and saved us from a feeling of isolation when encountering low days. Just knowing that we had a reliable conveyer belt of support was a huge asset, as everyone experiences the good and bad days together as a result.

> **Sarah Joyce** – good form today – cut and painted her nails.

> **Geraldine Joyce** – sick today, threw up all over the place but good form afterwards.

> **Geraldine Joyce** – great form, sitting on bed painting her toe nails black with permanent marker, but happy out, little minx.

> **Sarah Joyce** – good form, out home with me, back at bedtime.

> **Anne** – great day, dried up the dishes after dinner, says my dinners are the best, all smiles.

**Sarah and Ellie** – phone call from Mam. She is very, very distressed. Repeating, "I want to go home with one of ye". Cannot understand why we won't bring her out of here. Stripped of clothing completely and walked hallways, nurses got it hard to settle her.

**Geraldine** – good form this evening, ate her trifle, giving out to staff again today.

**Anne, Geraldine and Sarah** – in great form, lots of laughs, only speaks when prompted, most of it gibberish, untrue or silly. We asked her to name her children today, her response: Mary, Cait, Perry, Fork and Knife. (Probably forgets the question asked after a few seconds due to a fading short-term memory).

**Anne** – great form, smiling, told me to take home some logs for the fire as I was leaving her bedroom, she was pointing to the laundry placed on the armchair, funny. My response, no worries Ma, will do.

**Geraldine** – Mam said, not going to that dayroom anymore, the dinner is rubbish, steak and kidney pie, she is not buying any more furniture either.

**Anne** – Mam suspicious, ran the staff out of room, very cross and discontented.

**Sarah C** – thinks the staff are trying to get rid of her, ran the girls out of room again.

**Ellie, Sarah and Nanny** – jogged down to the shop for ice-cream – joke.

**Mike** – Mam is in good form considering she was out at Sarah's house for dinner, saying, Sandy the dog wouldn't even eat it!!! Joke, Mike winding Sarah up, I guess the dog is still alive.

**Sarah** –"idiot" (Sarah referring to above entry).

**Mary Joyce** – quiet but peaceful.

**Sarah Joyce** – great form, not asking to be taken out of nursing home, in the dayroom when I arrived, she is such a cutie. She said suspiciously, some strange lad comes in every so often called Mike, "tell him to get lost."

**Mike** – mother gets out of bed, presses green button – mother gets back into bed presses green button.

**Sarah Joyce** – asked at reception to have haircut, she said that the hairdresser charges a bucket load for a cut.

**Mike** – put mother to bed and sang a few songs.

**Sarah and Anne** – singing hymns, brilliant form, looks super although she has kidney infection once again.

**John Joyce** – Bread in tea "no cream", does not look well, the tea I mean, nanny in good form.

**Sarah** – trying to peel two apples, says I have to bring home the bits and grow some trees.

**Mary** – found her in dayroom eating the plants, in good form.

**Ger, Mike and Anne** – good form, says no point praying for Fergus (her son) waste of time he is a prod, lost cause.

**Mary and Jessica** – hi to all.

**John** – nanny lying back having a rest, in good form, had a lovely dinner in Sarah's house today, (great imagination).

**Sarah** – nanny wondering where the hell ye all are ????

**Anne** – I am studying trying hard to remember the four rules of the Health and Safety Authority, asked Ma for help. She says, "The Passion of The Lord is the answer". Ha, I wonder what the tutor might say if I gave this answer, probably get a big distinction for being original.

**Anne** – playing cards, Mam is cheating and feeling no guilt when corrected, just a slow moving bold smile on her face as if she is inwardly saying, up yours, melt your heart, she is a ticket, so so cute.

**Geraldine** – good form, made jam earlier.

**Sarah** – nanny can't find her watch, ring or remote for TV. Mentioned it to the staff. Said they will have a look.

**Mary & Ciara** – nanny in good form, chatty, tea and biscuits and then washed her Rosary beads in her glass of water before bed.

**Sarah** – neighbour was in for a visit, Mam told her to leave. Today she is in great form, all smiles.

**Geraldine** – Mam's clothes, biscuits and water all mixed up in bin, crumbs everywhere, in good form, she won €40 in bingo.

**Sarah** – in the dayroom pouring lashings of salt on her dessert.

**Sarah** – Two cardigans and two skirts on today. Very tearful but agreed to come outside to look at flowers.

**Geraldine** – suspicious, says the girls want her dead tonight.

**Geraldine** – tucked up in bed for night, says Barry (favourite grandson) is the only one that visits her – the ranch is yours Barry.

**Geraldine** – having her tea, now digging her sandwiches out of her tea cup with her fingers.

**Geraldine** – Ma says Anne is a little monkey for getting lost on the beach.

**Mary G** – unsettled, wants to go home, took her for a walk, distracted her until she settled, she is happy now looking through *Ireland's Own*.

**Geraldine** – very cross, but eating trifle now, so humour improving rapidly.

**Geraldine** – more trifle bribery, two layers of clothes on, hard enough to get one set off her to put her to bed.

**Mike & Fiona** – more bribes to get several layers of clothes off.

**Geraldine** – Four o'clock in afternoon, completely stripped in the bed, got her dressed and then down to dayroom for her tea, not a bit impressed.

**Mary G & Fiona** – very confused, in dayroom, refusing to eat her tea – went to the loo, all ok.

**Anne** – in brilliant form, played great cards.

**Mary G** – very confused tonight, tried to lift her with a sing song, no luck finding her rosary beads.

**Sarah, Anne and Lailah** – words all jumbled, in confused state when we arrived, tucked up in bed with tea and cake, now a little lighter in humour.

**Geraldine** – found her heading to the dayroom with bedside table instead of walker, smiling, in good form.

**Geraldine** – found her in shower room eating an orange.

**Geraldine** – Tried to escape earlier caught by Val and returned to cell.

**Sarah C** – spelling out words when asked questions.

**Geraldine** – has another UTI seeing doc in morning, looking through photo album says we are all saints today, Daddy is St. John.

**Sarah, Anne & Lailah** – she looks wonderful, new hairdo, not speaking though, in and out of bed like a jack in the box, all mixed up.

**Geraldine & Niamh** – knows our names, good form.

**Sarah** – Mam thinks her dad died today, so so so sad poor Mam. He died over 50 years ago.

**Anne** – Mam confused, says she wasn't out all day, said Sarah was supposed to collect her. But she was out at the hospital for her monthly infusion of antibiotics.

**John** – Mam would not get into her nighty for the nurse; she said she would try again later, looks good though, saying her prayers.

**Geraldine** – Ma said the girls just shoved her into the bed tonight.

**Mam** – 205 High + Tapping living….

**Sarah C** – good form, answering questions.

**Ger** – ate four bars of chocolate yesterday, am really cutting back now.

**Mike** – newspaper went missing again, mother washing rosary beads.

**Ger** – put Mam to bed, found her rambling through the corridors.

**Anne** – Mass, confessed all after jumping the queue, priest still in shock!

**Ellie** – I had a dance with Berty in dayroom, Mam enjoying the music, all good.

**Ger** – So tired, that's just me.

**Mam** – Prime drink, divide flowers.

**Sarah C** – painted Mam's nails, good form.

**Ger** – put her to bed, away with the fairies.

**Sarah C** – back from hospital, had fish and chips in my house, good form, giving out to Sandy, (poor dog probably wanted a chip).

**Sarah C** – Really bad form, skin very cold. Nurse took me to one side to tell me Mam is saying she is dying. I explained that the various medication administered may be making her forgetful, down and confused.

**Anne** – said she had another lousy day.

**Ger** – ate dinner now takes six sugars in tea.

**Ger** – slippers full of tissues. Fintan and Kathleen were in yesterday.

**Mike** – sitting on the side of bed after going to the loo. I asked her was there any smoke at John's house today at dinner; she said "No, I gave up smoking".

**Mam** – Barry Joyce, Clondulace, Portarlington, Co Laois

**Sarah Joyce** – asked to be taken to Auntie Cait's house on way home from the Hospital, she says Cait runs a boarding house.

**Ger and Sarah C** – in bed, says she is dying and ready for heaven.

**Mary and Ciara** – had tea and sandwiches, meds and two successful trips to the loo.

**Mam** – please put on your socks.

**Ger** – back from Mass, wants to go to school now.

**Anne and Mike** – in bed, told Mike not to bother coming to visit her again.

**Ger** – in bed early, she told "Berty to go to bed", so funny.

**Anne** – took Ma to Mass to pray for all ye sinners, she is busy now kicking a football about in the dayroom.

**Sarah C** – Mam in good form although cough still bad enough, wanted to know where all her other children are?

**Mam** – out to Mass Ger.

**Sarah and Ellie** – good form, two sets of cardigans on, put her to bed for a rest. Mike stop taking the paper home!

**Ger** – doc in, low dose of steroids, chest infection.

**John** – Mam is in good form, looking for a lift to Cloneygowan, needs to bring wet toast to Anne for dinner.

**Ger** – in bad form, wants to go home.

**Mary G** – bad form.

**Ger** – Touring all morning, wants out, dying again, I have to write to Perry and tell her.

**Sarah C** – shit day, wants out!

**Sarah C** – another shit day, wants to come to my house, won't go to Mass, there's a first.

**Mam** – Ger, twins, big arms.

**Ger** – in bed, no visitors once again. Don't know what that's about. Apparently my twins have disco arms.

# A distress text from Daron

My son Daron sent a text: "Come home Mam, nanny trying to leave the house." I sent a text back to him, "not to worry son, on way, will be about 10 minutes". I did not feel any panic, just amusement, thinking Daron's natural calm personality would be enough to pacify Mam if a problem arose while I was out.

When I entered the house Mam was livid, standing at the kitchen table with her hat and coat on. I had never been on the receiving end of her anger before. In fact I have no memory of her ever blowing a fuse or expressing anger. I did from time to time wonder how she was such a calm little Buddha or was she secretly building up a cart load of negative energy to generate power when we might run out of fuel.

The minute Mam caught sight of me she growled "How could you go to church without me?" I responded by saying, "Mam I just went to the woods for a walk with Eileen and thought you needed a rest". Unfortunately, Mam was incapable of comprehending what had actually happened and was fit to kill me. She looked wild and ready to attack, repeating the sentence several times with fire, "How could you have gone to church without me?"

The funny thing was that my sisters and brothers had been over for dinner with Mam. When leaving, Geraldine had offered to take her back to the nursing home. I figured that a rest might be the best course of action first. Up to this point if you suggested taking Mam back to the nursing home, she would swing her Zimmer towards the bedroom. It was always easier to take Mam back if she was well rested.

This was a Sunday, in the early stages of the Alzheimer's curse. I had helped Mam into bed for an afternoon nap after dinner. In general she would drift off to sleep within minutes and sleep for well over an hour. I decided it was safe enough to leave the house and get some air, as Mam was left in good hands.

Daron said that Mam had only slept for twenty minutes and had made her way to the front door unknown to him. He found her fully dressed with her coat, cap and Zimmer frame battling with the locked front door. It took a lot of persuasion to eventually convince her to walk to the kitchen where he made her a cup of tea. She was clearly agitated and determined to get to the church and had no more interest in tea than the man on the moon.

I had not taken Mam to the church that morning as she was clearly rattled and confused when I picked her up from the nursing home. I guessed she needed a rest more than Mass. Well after this confrontation I made a clear decision to make Mass a priority nevertheless. She was so insulted it was obvious she thought that I was trying to trick her. In reality, I was trying to recharge her batteries and to save her another trip around the bend with exhaustion.

It was right about at this point in time I realised it was a matter of making decisions day by day and being aware that there is no right or wrong. It is impossible to foresee whether or not the outcome  is going to be to her advantage or not. Needless to say she did not look in my direction or talk to me on the way back to the nursing home. She probably wanted to strangle me. We had taken Mam to Mass at every opportunity. It was sad to think that over the course of the next few months she would eventually lose interest in the Church and in prayer. Maybe at that point she had covered everything.

# A call from Sarah

My sister Sarah phoned. "Mam is depressed again, Anne. She wants to die. Will you come with me to the nursing home?" There were many calls of this nature from the nursing home in the early stages alerting us that Mam was inconsolable. She had written a letter to my sister in South Africa a few days before, repeating the words, "I am stuck", over and over. When she saw the two of us, she lit up and forgot her predicament.

We settled Mam into bed and took out the photograph albums which were a source of distraction in the beginning. When asked who the people in the album were, she had them all jumbled up. We didn't correct her. In her mind, the pictures of me are pictures of her and the pictures of her are actually pictures of her Mam, Granny Carty. So she has shifted back in time once again. When asked what age she is this day she said she is twenty-five and gives us a smile.

I read recently in a book that a mind which is affected by Alzheimer's is like a library in which each section of books will eventually collapse one after another like dominoes slowly and wearily on top of the other. The patient's short-term memory is the first to go. Then one segment after another disappears, from 80 to 70 to 60 and so on right back to birth. Jesus, we sit on the side of the bed fascinated that her mind has her way back in her 20's right now. Wouldn't it be great to look in the mirror, and see yourself looking like a young one? Maybe good old Alzheimer's has its positives. In fact, when she looks in the mirror she always looks pleased with her reflection. Well, Alzheimer's or not, Mam does look great at 82.

The feeling in the room has shifted to sweet and cheerful as we manage to get Mam distracted and singing for a while. I run my finger slowly under the words of the song in large print on a sheet of paper because I know that she cannot focus for long without the whole page becoming jumbled. We do not need an Alzheimer's college to tell us this – we know instinctively.

Mike, my brother, puts his head into the room after knocking first. It reminds me of Da who always did the same thing every time he came to the kitchen door at home years ago – he knocked first and then would laugh out loud when we would shout out, "Come in Da, we know it's you!". I guess another tradition lives on. Mike did this every night while visiting Mam, knocked, put his head in first saying with humour, "It's your favourite son". If Mam had company, his next words were always, "Now tell them who I am!" Her gentle response with a knowing smile always was "Mike!" Whoever was in the room would get a right kick out of this tomfoolery and fall around laughing. Which in turn made Mam smile and each smile was like another treasure to store. Even when Mam's speech became very limited she managed to say "Mike". Of course our brother liked to believe that he was her favourite but we knew differently – Mam just found his expanding head and smile a source of amusement.

We did love to see him arriving so we could make our escape and feel good leaving Mam in his care. Those were the nights we left the nursing home happy and could sleep with a clear conscience. There were many of these moments in the two years. Thank goodness for large families. Each good night's sleep recharged our batteries to face one more day with hope and enthusiasm.

# More tears swaddled in love

Today as we were leaving the graveyard, Lailah gathered a bunch of colourful stones bordering Da's plot and left them on the dash of the car. What a magical place for a small child to run around – it really must be a wonderland, filled with beautiful bright coloured stones, angel figurines, candles and flowers. Later, as we collect Mam from the nursing home while I was leaning over securing her seat belt, Lailah pushed past me squealing with delight, "Move over Mammy, I want to say hi to my Nanny." As she was doing so she spotted the stones from earlier and put them in Mam's hand saying sweetly, "Now Nanny I collected these for you at Granddad's grave today." As I placed Mam's Zimmer frame in the boot of the car, I heard Lailah say, "Have you got tissues, Ma? Nanny is crying".

There she sat, tears streaming down her cheeks, obviously saddened as she examined the little stones that had just dropped into the palm of her hand. Lailah's enthusiasm was then engulfed with concern as she mopped Mam's tears and hugged her to death as I searched in her handbag swiftly for a possible pacifier – a Rosary beads. We had become accustomed to singing hymns or saying a decade of the Rosary in the car to distract Mam on many occasions when caught in a conundrum. Looking back, the ritual of the Rosary was a bit like Mam making a cup of tea years ago as the resolution to all our little concerns. But now we were learning a few necessary life skills in relation to keeping things as light as possible for her in return. Mam did settle eventually. This is where the short-term memory being shot is a blessing at times.

Later that same afternoon, for the first time ever, Mam asked whose house she was in. Another new development. I didn't ask but am beginning to wonder sometimes does she know who I am. Looking back I was wearing a black trousers and a white blouse similar to the attire of the nursing home staff. Maybe this day she thought I was an extension of her nursing home care.

I wondered were these trips making her disorientated or was this just an off-form day. While I busied myself preparing dinner, I saw her look around with intense apprehension as if the surroundings were now strange. Out of the corner of my eye I noticed Mam throwing a towel across the room with a demented expression as if she was being taunted by somebody or something or maybe just pissed off at being lost with no purpose.

I try to no avail to lighten the atmosphere but I know that if I stood on my head and produced the sun, moon and stars it would not make a blind bit of difference right now. Mam was unreachable – her mind in an obscure grey place. The funny thing about the darkness is that sometimes it feels like a door has firmly been slammed shut stopping any light from getting through. Every day brought with it shades of darkness and light. There were times when I was just about to lose all hope and I would see a gentle flicker creep back into Mam's eyes as if she could read my concern and that that alone was enough to lift her out of this despair. Maybe it gave her existence some meaning.

# A little fairy with a magic wand

Out of the blue one day, the questions around family home visits were surprisingly answered and my mind was put to rest. Momentarily, at least. I entered the nursing home on this particular day and made my way to the opposite side of the dayroom to speak to another resident before connecting with Mam. While I was sitting chatting to this lady, I had full view of my mother. She was seated in her usual position looking miserable and engulfed with boredom. My sister, Sarah, had a day off work and had made arrangements to spend the afternoon with her. Sarah duly entered the dayroom full of the joys of spring, greeting everyone in her path. It would be hard to be down for long in my beautiful sister's company. She is a bright ray of sunshine.

The scene was worth watching. The very moment Mam laid eyes on Sarah her whole demeanour changed, gradually lighting up like a Christmas tree. Sarah got down on her hunkers and gently placed a loving kiss on Mam's cheek while offering her hands like an angel helping Mam to a standing position. Without further ado, she positioned the battered Zimmer for support. At the same time she courteously greeted the residents at the table, announcing sweetly that they were off out to lunch.

I watched mesmerised as the residents acknowledged this gracious greeting while observing this wondrous contented expression fall across my mother's face. It was like a little fairy had landed in that dayroom and waved a magic wand. I could feel all those hearts swell with delight as Mam willingly followed this devoted daughter like a queen bee to the car. It was a taste of freedom for a few hours.

Sarah would have boldly parked in reception for Mam's comfort if it were possible. I used to get such a laugh at the sight of that car in such close proximity to the entrance of the nursing home. It may have been a bit tricky for others to come and go, but our Sarah was determined to make it as stress-free as possible for Mam. I had the answer to that insistent question that continuously swirled around in my mind. Those excursions on good and bad days were invaluable up to the point when Mam's mobility became a real issue.

# Hoarding and hiding

While trying to get Mam into the car today we had a little tug of war. She would not let go of the Zimmer. It was like something straight out of a comic strip and I had a hard job holding back my inner giggle. I tried to explain that the Zimmer would be safe in the back of the car but she was determined to cling on to it for dear life. Eventually there was a distraction – thank goodness the neighbours arrived home from work. Her struggle was put on the back burner as she watched their car turn slowly into the driveway. She let go of the Zimmer willingly and settled herself into the car.

Wrapped around the top bar of the Zimmer was a towel she had taken out of my bathroom. I found her earlier rummaging around in the bathroom drawers after she had used the toilet.

This reminds me for some reason of the term "nesting" associated with expectant mothers, getting prepared for the baby's arrival. I think Mam was always preparing to escape. She was building up supplies and waiting for the moment someone might leave a door opened in the nursing home. Mam walked the corridors of the nursing home relentlessly trying to find a way to escape. She did this with great determination and a few times succeeded in leaving the building only to be returned to her cell as Geraldine used to say, with a smile. She was like a private detective always watching out for provisions and a clear exit. The other resident spectators said Mam would smile on her return as if to say, 'No worries, the next time I will succeed'.

Yeah, my mother without a doubt went through a stage of taking stuff left, right and centre. We found all kinds of things in unusual places. It was as if she was hoarding for a future calamity. What a surprise the day my hand landed on a sloppy mess while searching in her bag for a Rosary beads. Her Zimmer bag was the first port of call when something went missing. I reluctantly emptied the contents into the bin. There I found a concoction of tea, biscuits, oranges, and a thick sticky liquid that resembled jelly and ice-cream and happily swimming amongst the lot was her Rosary beads. On numerous occasions we found Mam sitting in her room with several layers of clothing. Hidden underneath those layers were pads, newspapers and stashes of tissue paper. A resident told me one day that Mam boldly leaned over and took a banana out of her wheelie bag while passing, explaining that she had to take a trip to the next village and it was going to be a long journey.

During the beginning stage of nursing home care, Mam also relished each morsel of food placed in front of her. She would have eaten the leg off the chair if it were possible. Dare anyone try to remove a plate before she is ready to surrender and their lives wouldn't have been worth living. This was uncharacteristic of her. While raising our family, Mam was always last to sit and eat at our kitchen table. All were taken care of before she lifted her own knife and fork.

One day a few months into nursing home care, as the staff were busy preparing for a religious ceremony, I glimpsed a lady with Alzheimer's at the next table holding her soup mug upside down high in the air, waiting and watching for the last drop of soup to slowly roll down to the rim. It was like something a child would do. She was not going to hand over that cup come hell or high water until satisfied. A staff member approached warily to take the mug but instantly met a litany of verbal abuse. In shock, the assistant turned on her heels and retreated without saying a word, quietly walking away.

It was interesting for me as I had watched Mam's character change dramatically at meal times. She was normally docile but the tiger in her appeared when she thought her grub was going to be threatened. I guess food may have been the only comfort when everything else faded into the back-ground – as independence and recreational activities don't fill the void for much longer. This fascination with food took a back seat like everything else until eventually Mam totally lost interest, her appetite diminished and the breakdown of her swallow made eating uncomfortable.

# Collect and return

I would be telling a lie if I said I approached the nursing home to collect Mam with ease at all times. In the beginning it was a joy because she was so chuffed to see one of us in order to get out. But the return trip was a constant nightmare as she tried every trick in the book to not go back. Then she settled for a period of time and the transition was smooth most days. But near the end, Alzheimer's took a good hold, seizing every fibre of her being, making her life miserable, whipping away her spirit and eventually her mobility.

There were times I did not want to see Mam lost, confused, terrified or broken. I pleaded with her to come back to her old self. In the very early stages she used to register a smile but as time went on, she would stare blankly into an abyss or shed tears of frustration. It got harder and harder to get a positive reaction. The only thing guaranteed to get a smile in the end was when one of us cursed wildly. In her Alzheimer's state she loved our boldness. Yet years before as children we would receive a sharp look for crossing that line. She could convey the kind of glance only women use when no knife is handy.

As I said, the return trip was worse than collection. I felt at times she sensed, correctly, that I harboured the feelings of a traitor. Even though I knew full well with Alzheimer's on board her ship, no person, place or thing was going to change those hours of vulnerability and despair. I also knew logically the enjoyment of daily activities and banter among the other residents would have been captivating for her had she been of sound mind. But still at times I felt riddled with sadness because try as I might on the really tiresome days, I had little power to alleviate her darkness. The only thing capable of changing her to a different emotional state was time and she had plenty of that.

I remember jumping into the car beside her one day to be met by an expression of sheer fright. Mam cried as she told me there was something evil in the car. Hours later she was still locked in that shocked state. God only knows what she had experienced. This condition robbed her calm and serenity and replaced it with fear, grief, isolation and a deep sadness.

Did it get easier? Not at all. I feel she was blessed in many ways to have had so many visitors. God knows there are many residents in care with no callers, no familiar faces to break up the day.

To give you some hope, there were many days when Mam arrived at my front door on her Zimmer. I'd say cheerfully, "So you decided to visit me" and she would give me a gentle smile. It was just the cutest thing. Believe me, each successful visit made up for all the uncomfortable ones, each smile replaced all the heartache. I guess those outings helped to break the monotony of her day in the nursing home. I believe with all my heart that each one of these excursions helped Mam remain linked, if only by a thread, to a fountain of unconditional love. In many ways having a big family was her blessing.

On more than one occasion, I did question those outings, wondering was it harder on her returning at the end of the day or did it meddle with her nursing home care routine. The feedback from professionals and other people at that time was to continue taking Mam out for as long as it worked. As I have said before, each Alzheimer's patient is different and so what works for one family may not be advisable for another. Mam was a calm lady before Alzheimer's and it was a pleasurable caring experience once she had plenty of rest.

My daughter, Lailah, aged between four and seven at the time was a brilliant help and distraction for a long time. She treated Mam like a doll, getting her fleece blankets, drinks, medication, and treats and playing endlessly with her. Originally, it was card games until Mam lost her concentration altogether and used to throw the cards down on the table. I remember on one particular return visit in the early stages Mam asking could Lailah stay with her in the nursing home.

It was at the latter stage that I regularly found Mam sitting hunched over, crying at her dining table. I would wipe her tears, take her to her room and cosy her up in bed for a nap. Most of the time I felt her energy was depleted from dehydration and sitting all day in central heating and having no purpose. After a spell of lying flat on her bed, she would usually drift off giving me the chance to leave her bedside and collect Lailah from school, hoping on my return she would be able for the trip to my house.

Before we knew it, her mobility started to seize up. Her movements became impossible, slow and tiresome as the messages to move in any way or direction were lost before any progress.

# A daughter's loving heart

Kidney infections, dehydration and viruses helped amplify Mam's confused state of mind and on some occasion caused hallucinations.

Her father passed away at harvest time in 1959 when he was in his sixties. Mam was 29 years old. She was only four years married with two small children and a baby in her arms when she received the news that Granddad had passed away. At that time Mam was expected to keep her new home and all this entailed including cycling many miles to her family farm to help out at harvest time. I can only imagine that after Granddad's ceremony, the loss was respectfully placed on the back burner for each to mourn in their own way and own time.

Recently I listened to a 93 year-old farming widow being interviewed about the hardships of country life years ago. When asked did she resent having to keep house and work the land, her answer was, "We hadn't time for introspection back then; we were all part of a unit". I am surmising that in those days of old, survival was top priority. Keeping the wolf from the door came long before allocating any more time than necessary to grieve for a loved one. It was a forward march at all costs.

In the following story Mam's "mind" is propelled back to

"fifty years earlier" and she has just received the news of her father's death.

The nursing home informed us there was an outbreak of the vomiting bug and that Mam had been in the firing line, was poorly, and dehydrated. She was only days over her monthly visit to the hospital for a two-hour infusion of bone straighteners and antibiotics, which alone was guaranteed to knock the stuffing out of her. You can just imagine our reaction when we received this news. We were duly advised not to visit the nursing home as care was needed to manage and keep the virus under control. A few days later my sister Sarah stood up from the dinner table with great determination and announced that neither hell nor high water was going to stop her going to the nursing home. She could not leave Mam without a visitor for another day.

Not too long after Sarah had left, she phoned to say Mam was in distress and could not be settled. Faced with this dilemma and against nursing home policy, Sarah decided to take Mam out to my house for a drive hoping that together we might sooth her. Over the course of the two years Mam stayed in nursing home care I witnessed many moving sights. But this one was like a scene from a heart-wrenching movie about a daughter's unconditional love and compassion for her mother.

Sarah parked that wintery afternoon at the entrance to my driveway. I found her sitting in the driver's seat when I approached, tears streaming down her face. Her heart was clearly broken because she couldn't take Mam's troubles away. Mam was sobbing inconsolably, grief stricken in the passenger seat holding Sarah's hand exhausted from the hospital treatment and dehydrated from the vomiting bug. I was standing at the door of the car watching the two of them crying. Through her tears Mam repeated the words "Daddy is after dying, Daddy is after dying." Mam was hallucinating. Her body was at its lowest ebb giving Alzheimer's the opportunity to turn back time and recall the memory of her father passing.

The amazing thing for me as a witness was the grief. It was so raw. There was no doubt Mam believed her Dad had just passed away. You could hear and feel the heartache radiating from the car. Sarah was devastated because she had the ability to feel Mam's pain. She did not try to water it down or convince Mam otherwise. She was wise enough to allow Mam be and hold her broken heart in her hands giving her time to emotionally settle with support and understanding.

A mother and daughter gelled together in sorrow is very moving. Sarah, bless her wonderful soul, sat there, a river of big sad tears running through laneways in her perfectly applied makeup. Imagine thinking she needed my support when well capable of soothing my mother all on her own. A mother's loving daughter, having no concept of her greatness. I was the privileged one on those occasions to watch this angel in action.

Looking at my sister I felt so proud. She could not leave Mam another day without a visitor and was right. Sarah had the determination to push the boat out and found a way to lift Mam's spirit by changing her environment and supporting her. Mam did begin to settle and her spirit started to rise as we chatted at the car. On that return journey to the nursing home my sister's heart could rest easy knowing that when Mam's head hit the pillow she felt loved and supported.

That evening I remember thinking Sarah deserved a gold star for her sensitivity. It was not the only time she went against the grain because she could not bear to think of Mam not having visitors. My mother's pain and grief was my sister's pain and grief. To look at Sarah in the car you would swear that Granddad had actually just died because of her consummate compassion.

Over the next few days Mam mentioned Granddad's wake and other neighbours who had passed away in her childhood. The mind is remarkable with its ability to rewind to earlier memories and believe it is actually that era. Sometimes I wonder is this the reason for Alzheimer's. Is it necessary for some to return to the past to release those unexpressed emotions of old and heal old wounds?

# Miss USA

I still tell people that my father did not remember our names as we got older. At the same time, he was getting older too and he had to cope with so much. In fairness to him, there was a lot of us, plus partners and grandchildren. He gradually learned to address us all by country, county, town or village. My sister Perry was called Ms USA, Mary was Mrs Kildare, Cáit was Mrs South Africa, Mike was Mr Emo and so forth.

After retirement, our parents moved into the modern world and installed a telephone. It was truly comical when either of them answered, Mam was so quiet she had nothing to say and Da? Well, he would greet the caller with a lot of volume and plenty of half-truths. When any one of his eleven might call home to speak to Mam, Da's response was always the same, "Your Mam is gone to the Galway Races", even if she was only gone to church or putting the clothes on the line. He was a scream. If either of my sisters living abroad took a notion to call home wondering if our parents were both still alive and kicking, Da would tell Mam when she entered the kitchen, "One of the foreigners rang". Mam would probably smile with relief as she was not interested in chitchat. The phone was for emergencies such as arranging her next card-playing event or enquiring about funeral arrangements.

Ms USA, although living abroad while Mam was a resident in the nursing home, must be given credit for her encouragement, wise counsel and gestures during this journey with Alzheimer's. In telling Perry about the heavy weight I felt at times finding Mam in a quandary, her feedback went something like this. "Anne, you must only visit Mammy when you have love and ease in your heart. If you go in rattled or feeling like shit, you will add to her discomfort and distress."

What a right kick in the ass this statement was at the time, but I knew it was filled with goodwill and love on my sister's part. Perry was right. I needed to hear these words as I did enter the nursing home at times with a heavy heart only to find Mam sinking fast in an ocean of despair and to top it off, a dark cloud hovering above me. Shame. I can promise it took all my reserves not to scream on those occasions. "Oh for God's Sake! Will someone please find a way to lift me Mam's spirits so I do not have to crawl under a rock and howl in the parking lot after this visit?"

Yes, you could say I was self-absorbed not realising that my expectation and lack of acceptance was actually causing Mam even more unnecessary grief. Little by little and step by step, I managed to crawl forward but it took a lot of effort. I increasingly became more aware and eventually learned to switch off emotionally and act in a more beneficial way towards my mother's care.

Even though I tried my very best to carry through Perry's wise counsel, I have to admit during some tiring transitions I fell backwards, allowing those ever-ready floodgates to have a field day and shoot open. I had no choice but to accept that this was the longing in my heart for Mam to have her senses back and find joy in her world once again.

There is little doubt that for most mere mortals it is "difficult to see the wood for the trees", when faced with one challenging situation after another. I guess to sum it all up, we must try to be aware of what we are carrying emotionally while at the same time being compassionate with ourselves as we trudge through the dark recesses of Alzheimer's.

I have to admit it was hammered into us right from the start that while tending to Mam it was of the utmost importance to understand that her carers must aim to become her communication bridge and, where necessary, to take action on the level least stressful for her. Sadly we discovered this was easier said than done with reason. As bigger mountains emerged over time they stirred up overpowering emotion, leaving no doubt that the heartache while climbing one hurdle after another may have been disadvantageous for me Mam.

Before long, we were to hit another brick wall as Mam slipped further back. She needed to be spoon-fed and toileted. We had to down tools and find a way through or over that wall. Little did I know that we would once again be rocked to our core, but like St. Theresa so wisely said, "This, too, shall pass". And it passed after many pitfalls. Watching our beautiful mother reduced to being treated like a child was not easy. We were torn apart. Mam's comprehension was fading rapidly, her once beautiful intellect was deteriorating. It's a struggle. Try as we may not to take over and diminish her independence, Alzheimer's was gaining power and was clearly winning the war.

# Feeding

In the dining room of the nursing home one day at dinner time, I remember finding some of the residents wearing adult size bibs, a larger version of the type infants wear. At that moment, my heart took a sudden dive. My overactive imagination immediately shot into fifth gear. I then began to secretly pray, "Oh for God's sake Lord! Spare my Mam". Although I had read and reread all the changes and stages, nothing prepared me for the actual reality of it all. Was I wishing Mam might just be exempt and skip a particular step or two for good behaviour, having outstanding patience with me Da and her eleven rascals for fifty years? God, we all knew only too well that in Mam's Alzheimer's-free years she prayed for Ireland. Surely she deserved a break. Thankfully, at this stage, she was still feeding herself and enjoying food, a blessing considering the joy was taken out of most other activities. My goodness. It is amusing to know about the never ending supply of hope we hold in our hearts.

The salt and sugar and other items had to be removed from the table as she would shake forever to sweeten her tea or spice up her dinner. She started to mess with the food and sometimes would take lumps out of her mouth to examine or disregard. Dare anyone annoy her or take the plate away until she was ready to hand it over. One day, months later, I popped in at meal time and there she was with a bib on. You can imagine the conversation I had with the gods on this occasion. I was inconsolable – my Mam was now officially at the baby stage. It was as if she had no idea what the food on her plate was for. Like everything else she gradually became disinterested in food and became childlike at meal times. Maybe that very first encounter with the other residents did soften the blow just a tiny bit. Otherwise I might have screamed, "What a ridiculous condition!" or, inwardly of course, some expressive expletives.

I remember being advised often in the early stages to be aware not to take over an activity unless totally necessary and allow Mam to remain independent for as long as possible. It was hard to sit back and watch while wondering when is "this moment", to yet again cross another line and take over. Gradually, feeding became a challenge. I would place a fork in Mam's hand and prompt her to feed herself. Mam would lift a massive amount of food onto her fork. There was no possible way this amount of food was going into her mouth. It would eventually fall off the fork and she would start the process over and over again. It was frustrating to watch. I did not want to take over. This is where one gets a proper sense of denial, watching, waiting, hoping that this is just an illusion, and if left to her own devices one day she will revert back and remember how to feed herself just like the graceful lady she was.

The time did arrive to take over and accept there was no going back. Fergus, my brother, was up from Galway to cook for our entire clan one Sunday in my house. By the time I got to the house after collecting Mam, the entire family of sons, daughters and grandkids had boisterously gathered in full force, full of laughter and chat. Mam sat cautiously at the head of the table looking around as if she was trying to get a handle on what was happening. She was looking as lost as she did first when I entered the dayroom.

When the dinner was ready to be served I sat beside her with a plate of mashed up dinner. She had no comprehension of what was happening. She was undoubtedly lost in the Alzheimer's tunnel. I tried to coax her to eat but she sat, blankly uninterested. After unwavering encouragement, she eventually opened her mouth and took a little bit of food only to hold it there, without swallowing. At some stage I was informed that the terminology for this stage is "pocketing". I am guessing that while her swallow was diminishing, the process has become uncomfortable or joyless. Somehow she managed to keep the food at the side walls of her mouth forever and no encouragement was going to move the process forward.

My sister, Sarah, walked into the kitchen, unware of what had taken place. She said confidently, "Let Mam hold the spoon herself", obviously thinking that I had jumped a stage prematurely. Then the penny begins to drop. Sarah sees Mam making no moves towards feeding herself. She, too, gives in and patiently starts to assist trying her living best to get Mam to eat. After mighty perseverance she realised there is no hope. Mam is in another land, staring, motionless with a look of desperation as if she is sitting amongst a bunch of strangers. My brother, John, gets fed up of us fussing, leans over the table, takes the plate of rejected food and smiles at us both.

It slowly dawned on me later that day. I had collected Mam just before they served dinner in the nursing home and maybe this is beginning to cause her unnecessary stress and confusion. Has she become accustomed to the daily routine, the sound of the other residents being assisted to the dining area, the buzz of the staff setting tables, the banter and chat of residents and care workers? Maybe they have become her new family. Is Mam lost among us now? What a hard question to have to ask oneself? Oh God, are we now pulling and dragging her like a rag doll unnecessarily in all directions thinking we are still of benefit? Another step we must consider is when would be the right time to withdraw. Would it be better to let her be? Perhaps our duty is to make her life as comfortable as possible and if these home visits are now of no benefit maybe it's time to step back.

As the weeks passed, Mam's health and swallow declined further. It was almost impossible to get her to open her mouth for drinks or medication not to mind food. Little by little, joy seemed to drain out of every pore as she had lost interest in meal times and everything else associated with living. It is impossible now to get any type of reaction. Even the little trifles Geraldine used to buy to lift her at night time have lost their appeal. Mam's energy and life force is almost non-existent. The only movement or communication now is when she puts her hand over her mouth to stop the feeding or drinking ritual. We have tried every trick in the book to encourage her. But nothing and no one has any power of persuasion. I guess it's time to let go and let God handle the rest.

# Letters for safekeeping

**M**am's diction and penmanship were superb. Even the weekly shopping list was a work of art. Her generation took pride in hand-writing skills.

The following letters belonging to Mam were saved thank goodness. Having her handwriting is like having a piece of her left to hold. It also shows through her writing how Alzheimer's affected her comprehensibility and spatiality in communication.

I wanted these letters presented before Mam's last visit to her childhood homeland to give an insight into her beginnings with her parents and ten siblings.

The opening letter was written by her on her first flight ever – to South Africa. It was sent to my sister, Perry, who was the adventurous one flying from one continent to another like a hen on a hot griddle. The trip to South Africa for Mam was to welcome another grandchild into the world. My sister Cáit living in Johannesburg asked Mam to visit for the birth of her second son Colin.

It was Mam's first flight at the age of fifty-seven and she describes this experience wonderfully. I was always fascinated at her ability to write so clearly and keep each line parallel. My sister, Perry, found this letter when packing up in the USA to move to the South of France to retire from retiring.

*Wednesday 3rd June 1987.*

*My Dear Perry,*

*Sorry for not writing before we left home anyway I hope you're getting on O.K. All were fine at home when we left TG, Cait, Brian and Davy are the best also. Mike, Eve and Barry left us at the airport Thursday and we flew out at 2.30, it wasn't so hectic from D to London and my ears popped a bit. We were to have a three hour stop over there but the plane was late refuelling and then they discovered a fault in the air conditioning, finally we left London at 9.30 – no problem – We had our tea shortly after ten and dinner about three am, all lovely and so well laid out, being my first flight it was a novelty and I thoroughly enjoyed it all – After a stop for refuelling we had breakfast at 10 am. – lovely too – in between times Mary and I played rummy and read a bit and after dinner played bonkers with a rancher who had been on a seven month tour of U.S.A, Scotland and England with his daughter.*

*We had centre aisle seats and had two empty seats beside us so we were able to curl up and sleep for about three hours. Cait, Brian and Davy were at the airport and saw us get off the plane. I was afraid they'd be gone as we were last out – my case had been left in Dublin and by the time all the luggage was gone and we'd asked at enquiries, it must have been over an hour, anyway they'd had a telegram to say my case would be sent next day and it arrived by Taxi Sat.*

*They live in a lovely place here about 2 miles from Johannesburg – 15K from the airport an end house in a Post Office complex so they have their own back garden. David is a lovely youngster, not a bit spoilt. Cait has her check-up today and hopefully it'll be the last before the baby arrives. We just went to the local shops Sat and yesterday into Jo. I bought the writing paper and postcards in the highest building in S.A. so we had a look over the whole place. It's all lovely, great scenery – the weather is gorgeous sunshine all day but I can't get used to it getting dark so quick, twilight at 5.30, dark at six – no local to go to so we have early nights. On Sunday David's baby minder Martha and her family were here and we had a Brie (like August Bar-B-Q). Hope all is going well for you.*

The second letter was written by Mam in the early stages of Alzheimer's, to my sister Cáit living in Cape Town with her husband and third son, Conor. Mam is enquiring about Conor. It is easy to tell she is confused and she mingles her message with a prayer, drawing a bridge and a gate at the end of the page covering a prayer.

*Dear Cait*
*How is Conor getting on*
*How is Conor*
*I hope he is Conor*
*Getting XXX*
*Love Heart, How is Conor getting. It's bring Conor to my mind*
*I know he's top of the hour Death*
*Amen*
*Mother pray for sinners*
*Pray for us now*
*Amen.*

In the third letter Mam refers to St. Bernadette, being stuck and where we live. This just shows her mind is not clear. She is once again mingling a message with a prayer. The message is unclear but at the same time it is obvious that Mam is trapped and held hostage by her enemy Alzheimer's. The letter starts off neat, but by the end is all over the place while she struggles for space on the page. Her writing is now tired and shaky.

*St Bernatt of Street*
*Pray for Meet*
*Stuck, Stuck*
*I'm stuck*
*Sweet Timetim*
*St, Time, St, Where*
*St Where Live*
*St, St, Beranat*
*Geraldine Tillage*
*On the Grace Where*
*We the whe we*
*Live, Im sweet*
*On the Sweet*
*Where wive out the hill*
*Outside*
*When we lived*
*Where_*
*The we lived*
*Join walking on the walking, on the*
*Where we used how used*
*Still where we lived*
*The Street when w live on the land*

*On start where we lived*
*Lived on Street where   on the where*
*We lived on the the   We lived on*
*Square lived on*
*The loved so*
*Mucked*
*Tweet where*
*Where we live So he on the street, landed where we*
*lived*
*Where*

The final letter was sent to Mam by her youngest brother, Dave, from her homeplace, Raheenakeera when she was working away in a different county many, many moons ago in 1951 at the age of 21. Dave was twelve years of age at the time and obviously a very caring soul as he signs off, "Your ever loving brother". I was thrilled to bits when Anthony, Mam's brother found this letter in a tin box in an outhouse on the farm some sixty-two years later and gave our family a copy.

Dave's writing skills and storytelling are exceptional for a young lad. He has the ability to open a doorway back in time and gives us a welcome glimpse into Mam's childhood home life. I wonder was his imagination wide awake because there was no technology back then for distraction. I am not sure if there was even electricity. Today, Dave, seventy-six years young, is a retired teacher living in Australia amongst his family of six grown up children and a delightfully extending clan under his belt too.

Letter to Mam, aged twenty-one, from her brother Dave, aged 12, in 1951.

Raheenakeeran
Geashill, Co. Offaly
13.12.1951

*Dear Nelly*

*Just a few lines hoping you are well as this leaves me at present. We are all well at home. Daddy bought seven pigs from Jim Conor. John is soon going to build a house. Jim, Daddy and John are in a woodwork class in the old school. Pat Dunn is in Hospital. He was operated on Wednesday. Billy Murry sold his farm. He got 2000 pound for it. Cait and I got needle on Thursday, Diptera.*

*John bought five cattle in the fair Friday. He paid twenty five pound a peace. Dicky Mangan gave us a goose for Christmas. Liam got a new motor car a few days ago, he takes very good care of it. Jim is making a wash stand in the woodwork class, Daddy is making a dresser. John is making a table, Daddy is building a new cow house. I bring the milk to Kavanagh every morning. I will be expecting a Christmas box from him at Christmas. John has the house nearly drawn away. We got the potatoes and mangles saved.*

*Anthony and Brock like going to Port school. There is a silver circle started in Port, Anthony is a promotor in it. Seamus Corcoran won five pound on his card, Anthony got ten shillings for helping him. Mammy sold four turkeys and kept one – she got ten pound eight shillings. The four of them weigh fifty eight pounds. Mr Kavanagh is building a new shop. I think I have all the news told to you needing mind my* scribbling because I was hurry because mammy was going to iron. I will be expecting a long letter from you at Christmas.

With best wishes
I remain your loving brother Dave.
X X X

# The summer request

Today was a good one. I took Mam out for a visit. The transition from the nursing home was relaxed and peaceful. Easy to tell she was pleased to see me as I received a gentle smile. Another one to treasure. It was one of those sweet perfect days of summer sent straight from the heavens – blue skies and sunshine accompanied by a warm gentle breeze.

Mam sat on the big old wooden swing, my sunhat on her head and a fleece covering her knees. I laid a plate of cream cakes on the ledge within hands' reach and went back into the kitchen to make her a cup of tea. When I looked back over my shoulder, Mam was blissfully licking cream off her fingers. After the picnic we sat together in comfort while she coloured a picture with Lailah's twistable crayons, a wonderful invention, one of the plusses of the modern world. My mother was a beautiful writer and it was no wonder that she coloured each section with precision and gentleness. I sat with her gladly handing her the different colours and showing interest. Otherwise, she would just put the stuff aside and sit staring blankly into space.

I clearly remember her looking out from under the rim of the sunhat and quietly asking me to take her home to Raheenakeeran, her birth place. This was the first and only time Mam made this request. I was taken by surprise as at this point Mam had difficulty verbalising. She certainly had not been able to make a request or string a sentence together for over a year. I guess we were all a little bewildered at the fact that during the early stages Mam never asked to go back to our home where she cared for eleven children and Da for over fifty good years. Maybe the heart went out of it after Da passed away. Well, for whatever reason, Mam was just about to skip the childrearing stage and head right back to her own roots, to her beginnings where she was cradled in the arms of her own parents as a child. A nicer thought I think.

Anthony, who is Mam's younger brother, and his wife, Patty, still live in her original home place. This home remained the hub of the Carty family as each member branched out to build a new nest but gravitated back time and time again to "Granny's kitchen" for support and advice while they reared their own children. Wasn't it the done thing years ago for a family member, usually a son, to marry and follow in his father's footsteps working the land once the parents had passed, whilst keeping the door wide open and a hand of welcome out to the other members? It is a true blessing to have experienced this old world of connection and care, coupled with a cup of sweet tea and brown bread while our shiny new world of fast cars and technology leaves little time for kindling those important fires of support.

A few days later I kept my promise and brought Mam for the last time to Raheenakeeran. I took a road that I didn't know because it was closer to the nursing home, a route that Mam would have known well but I had little experience of. Going astray had a fine chance. Nevertheless we hit the road with eagerness and cluelessness and we got lost. Now we are only talking about travelling approximately eight miles of country roads but I had to give in and flag down a car to get back on track. Lo and behold, we arrived at the head of the driveway which is now recognisable as the entrance to the local soccer club where a sign at the entrance has been conveniently placed. A blessing for us. I pointed out houses along the way that would have been very familiar belonging to Mam's brothers and childhood neighbours. She had no idea that her family and neighbours resided within. She was lost in her own homeland.

To my amazement when we arrived at Anthony's door, she recognised her brother and his wife Patty. It is true what they say, home is not the bricks and mortar – it's a feeling. We were all beside ourselves with delight at the instant recognition of her sibling and his wife. These are the most wonderful people in the world and words could never describe the warmth and welcome we received when we entered the house. It was like Mam was totally precious. I bet they felt deep down our loss of our mother and their sister to this condition.

It is a wonder in this rat race of a world that there still remains in our psyche, our connection to our roots, recognition of care beyond words and an unbending feeling of family ties. If Alzheimer's had not presented itself, these little excursions would never had happened or would not have had the impact of exposing our longing to reunite with our family origins.

That day we were showered with a welcoming and delightful feeling as Mam sat quietly soaking up the atmosphere like an amused child, drinking tea and gathering up the cakes. Nobody passed any remarks.

During the visit Mam's nephew arrived. I can still feel the energy between them dance as he moved towards her. It was an instant loveable recognition as she sweetly addressed him by name, "Martin". With the exception of her saying 'No' to her knowledge of directions and homes along the road earlier, she otherwise sat amongst her care clearly contented, drawing every moment in.

Patty shared with us delightful memories and photographs of her sons' weddings before we made our way back to the nursing home. Mam never spoke another word nor did she ask to return to her homeland. Maybe somewhere inside she was quietly saying goodbye.

# Toileting

This is the only way I can describe toileting. Each person is born, develops awareness and is trained to observe and conform. Then, if unfortunate enough to be diagnosed with Alzheimer's, there is a gradual stripping away of the memory right back to its beginning and a weary decline of all conditioning takes place in preparation to exit this world. Then there is a return to the sod, to leave the very same way you arrived with a clean slate free from labels and the pressure to conform to the adult world.

It is difficult entering into each new stage of Alzheimer's but as with everything in life, one begins to flow with it in due course after many trials and errors. This is not something that takes place overnight. It's a gradual and sometimes stressful process. After finding Mam damp or soiled on many occasions, incontinence pads had to be introduced. Then came pull-ups and finally a complete pad similar to a baby's disposal nappy in adult size.

This was another setback for Mam and I can tell you she did not take it lying down. There were many pads hidden, taken off and binned, put in the toilet and thrown at the nursing home staff. Eventually Mam got worn down and gave up the fight, retreating and then taking one more reluctant step into that crazy world.

Believe it or not, toileting was not really as much an ordeal as watching Mam lose more and more of herself within this dark Alzheimer's tunnel. Lots of those toileting moments were magical because time stood still and the outside world took a back seat. I learned patience and the meaning of living in the moment. I was forced into Mam's world where Alzheimer's had control of the gear stick and I had no say in the matter. I am so grateful that Mam not only was our anchor but also an angelic parent with oodles of grace, calm and patience while rearing us eleven. She deserved a positive approach with care. There was no rushing this process and if the business was done without a hitch it was like winning the lottery.

As Mam moved into the next phase it was harder to keep her on the toilet long enough to do her business. She might try to get off half way through the process unaware that her bladder or bowels were just about ready for action. It was not a pretty sight.

I learned to be organised very quickly: a plentiful supply of baby wipes, pads, face/bum cloths, kitchen towels, creams, gloves, plastic bags and a change of clothing always at hand. But of greatest important were music sheets with all the old songs in large print. These songs for a long time distracted Mam as she might attempt to sing which in turn encouraged her to sit on the toilet long enough to complete her business. It was really no different than a mother finding ways to amuse her toddler while introducing toilet training – a mother will use every trick in the book until the process eventually registers.

Sooner or later, like with every other endeavour, 'Amazing Grace' and 'Danny Boy' got worn down and after a short verse into any song she would throw the music sheets at me indicating that she had enough and was getting bored. As soon as she was seated she wanted to be lifted and it was only luck at this stage that she used the toilet at all. The funny thing was afterwards as she stood at the sink in front of the mirror there was always this look of surprise as if she was pleased with her reflection while she washed her hands. This little smile, knowing she was oblivious to what had just taken place, was enough to reignite understanding once again, making me see the funny side of it all.

As time moved towards the last stage, toileting became almost impossible, although we were well aware that given instruction and getting a response would take time and perseverance, getting Mam to sit on the toilet was sure to test the patience of any saint. After coaxing and encouraging her as far as the toilet she might turn around and back up. Just as you thought you were about to make progress she would move forward again forgetting why she was there, circle, go back towards the toilet once again, turn around, back up and finally move forward again.

This was not something that happened with speed; it was all in slow motion. This is about the point in time that we had to accept that Mam would probably no longer be using the toilet. But it was much too sad to accept or say for certain that using the facilities was well and truly over as, once in a blue moon, when she backed up she actually did sit and complete her business. Those moments were now few and far between. In the end just like a baby, Mam would fill her nappy in company unaware I am sure of what was going on. The Alzheimer's patient then has no concept of privacy; they are unaware of what is taking place within themselves or in their immediate environment. I guess the dos and don'ts, the rights and wrongs, appropriate timing, embarrassment and meaning have long since gone underground.

# In the house of the Lord

The very first fright happened when Mam got back on her feet after her hip and wrist operations. I coll-ected her from the nursing home to take her to church. Just after the priest gave her Holy Communion, I heard her stomach rumble like a volcano and she began to break wind. I leaned over several times asking her to follow me to the toilet but she just turned her head away with a look of total confusion.

How astute one's senses become when panic sets in. You know what they say: "The worst part is the anticipation or the knowing that there is going to be an explosion". I knew then without Mam's cooperation I was going to have to suck it up, excuse the pun. I had this vision of the people surrounding us and moving quietly and discretely to a safe refuge out of harm's way. Thank God the service ended and the congregation moved towards the exits. I took Mam's arm gently and guided her towards the toilet area which was a bit of a trek from our seat and I prayed to all the angels and saints, for time.

I'm afraid, we did not make it to the toilet on time. It was not a pleasant scene but thank goodness there was nobody else in the hallway heading to the toilet. It came out of Mam with almighty force and I can still hear her gentle voice saying, "Oh", I reassured her and continued to guide her towards the toilet as if nothing was happening, then seated her gently on the loo. I looked at her and said, "I have to run to the car to get supplies, please don't worry I will be back". I took off like a bat out of hell hoping that she would not follow and slip on the floor as it was well and truly soiled.

It is safe to say the parishioners remaining must have thought the church was on fire because of the speed I passed them to get to my car. I threw open the boot, grabbed my bag of supplies and returned to the crime scene as one might say. God love Mam, I'd say she didn't even miss me I was that fast. She looked up at me from where she sat innocently like a little child and said, "Oh Dear". All I have to say at this point is that my heart filled with love and empathy, she was so gracious, patient and pleasant. True to her nature.

I cleaned the hallway, the toilet floor, and her shoes before taking them off in order to remove her clothes. I thanked the Lord for modernisation and the genius who invented baby wipes, kitchen towels, pads and throw-away plastic carrier bags. I was so grateful that I did not have to involve another in order to preserve Mam's privacy and dignity. Not that she might have noticed, but I had that need to protect her. By the time I got her back to the nursing home she had long since forgotten the ordeal. I was in a state of amusement at the fact that just that very morning I had put a bag of supplies in the car, intuition or good luck, who knows. What in the name of the heavens would I have done otherwise?

# The bed

Today was one hell of a test. I found Mam sitting on her bed in the nursing home looking through her prayer book. There was a foul smell in the room, but I figured she had just been to the toilet adjacent to the bedroom. I reached over opening the window the allowable gap, hoping to clear the air. I could see that she was overdressed but I didn't fuss. She was beside herself with delight because I had arrived. I helped put on her raincoat while she was sitting, gathered up her belongings and started walking with her towards the exit, only then realising I'd left the car keys on the dressing table.

I knew at this stage it would have upset and confused Mam to head back in the same direction. I asked an assistant to continue with her towards reception as I retrieved the keys. I re-entered her bedroom and to my horror I found the bed spread where she had been sitting was badly soiled. I gathered it up, grabbed a laundry bag and ran towards the car realising there was a good chance that her clothes were also destroyed. I then discretely placed a protector on the car seat just before Mam got in and drove her home. After entering the house, I directed her straight into the bathroom finding the seat of her skirt stained badly and fit only for the bin. It was mind baffling as the skirt inside and out was badly soiled. Given that the fabric was non-porous, this could only mean one thing. She must have done her business on the bed, put on her skirt and sat down in the same spot to say her prayers.

She could sit there content until the cows came home unware of the predicament and no apparent sense of discomfort or embarrassment. Jesus, I was utterly flabbergasted. Although I was grateful now for the advantage of memory loss, I was truly in bits, feeling Mam was basically in another world exposed and vulnerable, open to whatever lay ahead as Alzheimer's appeared to have the upper hand and was clearly having a field day.

Given that Mam was totally oblivious to the mess, she was amazingly tolerant and graceful allowing me to strip, wash and re-dress her. When she was settled and out of earshot, I reached for the phone to inform the nursing home about the situation. Amazingly, I was able to care for Mam with calm and reserve but when I was free to redirect my attention to this new task, I suddenly wanted to run back into the bathroom and throw up, my stomach and heart heaving with sadness and shock.

My hands trembled anxiously as I scrambled through the directory, while a volcano of hot and distasteful anger smouldered away behind my rib cage. I felt let down. I felt Mam was let down and I was left wondering were there blurred lines on care especially for Alzheimer's patients. Had we made a huge mistake? Had we put our beautiful mother in an institution with much too high of an expectation?

The sound of the phone ringing shocked me right back to earth and put the brakes on my overactive imagination which now was doing somersaults. I wanted to know there and then why I found Mam in this mess; I wanted someone to tell me this would never happen again, I wanted to wake up from this nightmare and realise that it was just an infuriating dream.

The nurse on duty did not seem surprised and needed time to investigate, eventually getting back to me explaining that the care assistant on duty around that particular time said she had tried her best to put a pad on Mam that afternoon but was met with resistance. She then proceeded to list the number of times Mam had been basically overseen. I guess all the boxes on the chart in front of her had been ticked. Was my Mam now just a number? She could not see the tears of frustration running down my cheeks. Maybe she did sense I was about to break, but kept it professional in order not to deal with anything other than information.

I needed a warm heart as I felt isolated on the other side of a brick wall much too high to climb. Oh God! What has this world come to? Instruction, paperwork, showing up at a door at a particular time? Yes, of course, I knew somewhere deep within that nine out of ten healthcare professionals approaching Mam and the other residents did so with loving hearts and a knowingness. Looking back, this was just one of the off days, but do you think this rationality had a place to rise in my being? No, it was now well and truly shoved down beneath a swamp of unshakeable distaste and anger. I wish at the time I had had my father's balls and his words if he had been still alive, "Let the God damned gates of that swamp open and scream 'Wake up' for Christ's sake".

I was left feeling Mam was on a check list. I needed someone to place a plaster of kindness on my broken heart and address my despair or try at least to reassure or prepare me for the journey ahead, good or bad. Every cell in my body was aching so badly as I despairingly yanked back each tear with resolve. Mam was still very much a person of importance in our world and we needed to find a better way. If this outcome was inevitable, why were Mam's carers not forewarned at the stage of finding pads hidden in funny places like in her cardigans.

The mind is a wonderful thing in the way it can memorise and assess situations. Days later when the fire began to dampen, I recalled seeing a lady with a look of dismay leave Mam's room on the day of the incident. As she looked like a doctor, I also remember wondering will I approach her and ask her how she found Mam. I had never seen this member of staff before and presumed she had no time for chit-chat as she did not address me or look in my direction. Weeks later I realised she was actually a care assistant, new on the block therefore maybe not having the wherewithal or experience to explain the complexities of this transition.

My mind was blown clean away in those first few encounters. I still remember the feeling of despair as I drove towards my house that day. Even knowing that Mam's brain function was diminishing further and she thankfully had no memory, it did not take away the disappointment. This difficulty was always going to be hard to accept on any level even with logic. Who wants to find a loved one in a saturated or soiled position and to top it all, because of recurring infections at times, a foul odour to accompany this predicament? Wasn't this one of the reasons Mam was handed over to professional care? To understand each Alzheimer's patient and where they are at each stage of this journey, I guess it is inevitable that for everyone involved there will be many pitfalls and adjustments.

Alzheimer's or otherwise, there is a want in all of us to find our loved ones in a clean environment happy and smelling of roses. I guess just like us, Mam's medical team were faced with the same dilemma. They had to assess and reassess Mam time and time again as to the amount of assistance needed at each stage of this condition in order to allow her to remain independent for as long as possible before making other changes for her comfort and well-being. Maybe there was no other way around this dilemma unless Mam had someone sit by her side 24/7 which would be unrealistic and would amount to the same thing, adjustment and acceptance.

A baby is automatically placed in nappies from birth, moves towards pull-up pants and finally underwear. Even with a toddler it is hit and miss. One day a parent will feel they have won the race only to find that it is a three steps forward and two steps back undertaking. Trial and error. Just as the parent is about to give up, miraculously out of the blue, the penny drops and the child takes the next step towards independence. To move through the reverse stages with an Alzheimer's sufferer must undoubtedly be much more challenging and in most cases a road paved with many stumbling blocks. There is no awareness or logic as time moves forward, or should I say backwards, and the person with Alzheimer's eventually becomes dependent.

In order to march on, we carers must also be supported and allowed time to emotionally adjust before the fog clears as we gradually gather our thoughts and experiences together in order to gain the ability to see a broader picture and put these trying steps into perspective.

I guess the majority of people are completely raw just like us, having no previous knowledge of this condition. It is unrealistic to expect a knowingness before it has unravelled. It is putting the cart before the horse.

# Seán's passing

**M**am's brother, Seán, still independent and in good spirits, died just on the edge of his 90th birthday. His nature was similar to Mam's – quiet, peaceful and easily pleased. He was blessed to live with his son, John, and his wonderful family for many years. Because of this he experienced Heaven long before his calling.

There are questions hanging over us at that time: "Do we tell Mam her brother has just passed away?" "Will she understand or will it blow her away?"

I drive with anticipation to the nursing home in order to go to a Sunday service. I find Mam in her bedroom weary and stiff in a world of her own. I know instinctively it is not the right time as her comprehension is poor; each movement needing clear guidance. It is an absolute struggle to get in and out of the car. I have no choice but to park right at the church doors. Thankfully, Lill, who is Mam's sister, was in the church and she walked Mam up the aisle to a seat.

As the church service began I started to feel a little anxious. One part of me sensed a duty to tell Mam of Seán's demise and the other part wanted to save her the grief. I knew the priest would eventually announce funeral arrangements. I sat there in a quandary wondering would Mam be aware enough to receive this news. Mam floated in and out of sleep throughout the service. The priest announced Seán's arrangements, not once but twice, but Mam did not notice or make any comment. She was much too wiped out to be tuned in.

Immediately after the service the congregation started to gather around Lill to commiserate. I stood behind quietly indicating with care that Mam had not been told the news. They respectfully understood. There is an absolute beauty to Mam's generation. They are so wise and honourable. Their gentle expressions alone have the capacity to speak volumes.

I could feel Mam's exhaustion as we drove afterwards to my house where she once again drifted in and out of sleep before and after lunch. When she eventually received the news of Seán's passing, her response was natural but surprising, "Oh, may he rest in peace". When asked if she would like to attend the wake, she immediately without hesitation replied, "Yes" with such clarity it was unbelievable, considering that only hours before, she had been definitely in no man's land.

She sat willingly into the front seat of the car quietly wiping tears from her eyes as we prayed for her ease and peace of mind on the journey to see Seán for the last time. This was one of the sweetest, emotional scenes I ever witnessed; it was as if Mam had been granted a break from Alzheimer's and that her old self had come back to us for a few hours.

This brother and sister could have been twins in nature, cut from the same cloth, gentle and pleasant. They never made announcements or talked unnecessarily but somehow you just knew their importance and the wonderment of their pleasant souls.

As we entered the room where Seán lay, Mam started to cry. She looked like she was about to collapse with grief and family members gently guided her to a chair. Little by little her remaining brothers and sister entered the room. The door was respectfully closed and God's heavenly angels may have descended there was such serenity in the room.

Mam's brother, Jim, looked compassionately across the room dropping his head and humbly prompting his sister to start the Rosary. We then got a glimpse of Mam before Alzheimer's took hold. When she spoke, her words were clear, gentle and emotional. She moved through each decade of the Rosary graciously. In her grief and sadness there was an outstanding beauty, a feeling of true love and a connection to her family. There was also an unexplainable feeling of wonder. I have no doubt everyone felt it. How did my mother lead in prayer when she barely had two words to rub together in previous months? It was inexplicable. God must have granted her a passing reprieve.

On the journey back to the nursing home that evening, Mam, referring to the coffin, asked quietly, "Is there a lid for the box?" She asked the same question on the following day on the journey to the funeral. In the church during the service she asked with curiosity like a child was Seán actually in the box.

It was a beautiful end-of-life service but unfortunately the heavens opened up just as the service ended and was accompanied by a vicious wind. Hail, rain or snow, Mam was adamant about attending the burial. It was that look of desperation and disappointment when we reached the car that softened our hearts. We had no choice. We wrapped her up in blankets and struggled with umbrellas to shield off some of the crazy elements while escorting her down to Seán's grave. Bless her determined gentle soul, she got her wish to bid her brother farewell with love and prayer.

That evening, after returning home once again, Mam boldly snuck Lailah's food off her plate at teatime. Without warning, we were all thrown right back in at the deep end. I just smiled at her because it reminded me of my brother doing the same thing when we were children, snatching sausages off one another's plates. Mam had that very same look of victory as Lailah's displeasure registered. What an exasperating world we live in.

# Lost among others

I walked into the dayroom of the nursing home today to find Mam slumped forward onto her table weeping. This had become a regular occurrence in recent weeks. Maybe an old Irish tune has triggered memories from her past. Maybe the utter boredom is breaking her down. Maybe she just needs to lay her head down. Tears are streaming down her cheeks, her nose dripping onto the table; she is lost among others in this busy dayroom.

I am devastated for her, the sadness latches onto every single cell of my being and it takes everything within me to stop myself pulling up a chair to join her in her despair. As I look up I catch the eye of a 91-year-old resident sitting at the next table. It is easy to tell she is also willing my mother some comfort as she gives me that knowing gaze: "God bless your Mam." I reach towards the dispenser for some tissue to clean her face and gradually help her to stand. She falls willingly into my arms where I stand for what seems like an eternity hugging her hoping to squeeze some of that sadness out.

The tired old Zimmer is in front of Mam and I guide her gently towards the bedroom. En route she tries to enter rooms belonging to other residents. She is lost. We settle together on her bed where at times this would cheer her up or make her smile but she looks at me in desperation, her lips quivering as if she is trying to tell me something. It is obvious her cup is overflowing with hopelessness. How can I expect her to feel differently? I know only too well that Alzheimer's has robbed her of any solace. Unless it loses its power, we can expect more of the same.

Dear Jesus, I ask myself, am I capable of bringing any peace to my mother's mind and heart? What I do know is that a rest may ease her despair but I am afraid she may have done too much today. If she were able to communicate, she would probably ask the staff to help her to bed early in the afternoons before becoming exhausted. I know it is unrealistic to expect the staff member to sit with her and hold her hand all day and night, especially when there are times the despair is unshakeable, but it is heart-wrenching to find a loved one surrounded by people, feeling so miserable. I feel caught between the devil and the deep blue sea.

On the one hand I am frustrated, wanting to scream at someone and on the other hand I know that lately when Mam dwells in the darkness sometimes she is past the point of rescue and is unreachable.

She is much too agitated to sleep right now and after some time I try putting face cream on her. She promptly slaps my hand away with force. You know what they say – any reaction is better than none at all. I wonder. I can hear the bustle of the other residents in the corridor making their way to the dining area. It is teatime. No need for a clock in this establishment. All one needs to do is listen.

We return to the dining room. It is obvious Mam does not even see the other residents or staff. Their greetings float way above her head as there is no meaning in her dark world. I try to reach for a light at the end of the tunnel and at least be grateful that she must, even if minimally, be in a better state now than two hours earlier. But there is another voice in my head saying, "bullshit". I turn on my heels feeling crushed as a care assistant with a little skip in her step approaches Mam's table. There is no acknowledgement from Mam, not even a flicker of interest as she stares into the unknown. This evening's meal and the promise of help hold no significance. If the assistant has angel gloves, Mam just may cooperate for a moment or two before lifting a hand to indicate an abrupt end.

I cannot face saying goodbye. I know without reservation that I have not made one blind bit of difference. She is unreachable, lost once again amongst others. It is soul-destroying.

I compose myself and exit feeling a complete failure. I hate this shit condition. It is ridiculous. I just about make it to the car park and find myself as I found my mother a few hours earlier, slumped over, tears streaming and my nose dripping, pleading with the Lord to take her or give her back her peace.

Maybe that's exactly what Mam was doing when I found her a few hours earlier. Maybe she was begging for mercy.

# Another assessment

The doctor called this morning to let us know Mam had been assessed again. She had become more withdrawn, disinterested, and non-responsive. A decision had been taken to cut back her medication and the alarm bracelet had also been removed.

It is safe to say she will never try to escape again. I had read recently that Alzheimer's medication should be withdrawn if it is having no therapeutic effect, if the patient is no longer able to recognise family members, is losing the ability to do anything for themselves and needing more and more personal care.

The doctor advised to watch for signs of change and to introduce ourselves now whilst visiting to save Mam getting frustrated as she tries to remember names. At this stage we were also to be aware that it may not be of any benefit for her to spend time outside the nursing home and to therefore cut back gently on these trips.

I was beginning to feel myself that she was less comfortable with life outside and that the ordeal of moving from one place to another was becoming a challenge. Each journey meant a series of instructions. It was beginning to become unmanageable. Taking a step forward involved an immeasurable amount of time, patience and perseverance. For a short while, after cutting back on the meds, we noticed a difference. The drowsiness seemed to dissipate and Mam became a little more alert. She appeared brighter and we were able to manage the outings once again. But this change was short-lived.

A year and a half now living in nursing home care and Mam has begun to ask when out on these dwindling visits, who owns this house. She is retreating further and further. I wonder some days does she even recognise me or anyone passing through. Today when I picked her up she looked rattled and was crying, repeating the words, "I am dead". Thank goodness for my calm son who was in the car at the time. He said "Dead tired, Nan, needing a good rest". Mam didn't pay any heed and continued to weep. I am sure my son wasn't too far off the mark. At least his input lightened my mood.

While on the medication, Mam's senses were dulled and the withdrawal changed her demeanour once again from withdrawn to alertness. Now it was evident that these transitions had made her exhausted. It was like she was being thrown around like a rag doll from one state to another. I truly sensed her despair and felt like crying with her. Going through this with Mam has made me aware of the trials patients go through to find a suitable prescription with the right amount of medication for each individual to stabilize. It must be harder with Alzheimer's as the patient hasn't the ability to monitor their own feelings or well-being in order to give feedback and have the level dropped, heightened or changed completely.

I lay quietly beside Mam on my bed as soft tears ran down her cheeks while she thumbed the pearls on her Rosary beads until eventually she settled emotionally and drifted off. I then got up and snuck out of the room like you would after getting a child to sleep hoping that the movements would not disturb her. Sometime later I glanced into the bedroom to find her in a calmer frame of mind and the colour gently returning to her cheeks.

Lailah spent the rest of the afternoon encouraging Mam to take little sips of water through a straw and as evening arrived her mood had changed for the better. Mam was now able to cope once again. There is no doubt lots of rest is key at this stage, as even sitting upright tires her out.

# The end of the road

Taking Mam out of the nursing home had become trying. I lived for moments of ease or calm hoping they still served a purpose and that on some level Mam was still getting a little joy from these breaks. But there were no positive moments, there was no action or reaction. I think if a bomb exploded in my kitchen right now, Mam would be none the wiser.

Today she sits beside me, motionless. I try endlessly to get liquid into her to no avail. I give her a paint brush and some paper but the brush remains upright in her hand. I try my best to draw her out but she stares ahead lost and bewildered. As evening approaches, it is as clear as crystal that these visits are more than likely coming to a close. She is stuck in time, like someone has pushed the pause button.

In order to return to the nursing home, she must be gently encouraged to a standing position and then helped with her coat, hat and scarf before she makes her way very slowly to the front door.

She is very slow but determined to reach her goal, "the car", knowing the route well as the instruction finally registers. As she nears the front hallway, her bladder empties and although wearing a pad, the force sprays liquid everywhere, down her tights into her shoes as a steady warm puddle forms around her feet. I know that I have no choice but to peel each layer of clothing off, wash her down and start again. But she will not now be deterred from her mission.

Oblivious to the fact that her bladder has just relieved itself and that she is much too damp to step out on this winter's night, it becomes a battle of wills and takes all my strength to stop her from moving forward. I have no choice but to stand in front of the Zimmer and place my foot firmly on the bar. I start to remove Mam's coat while trying to reassure her that we only need to stop for a short while. Unaware of the dilemma, she is still in her mind heading through the front door and has no idea why I am holding her hostage.

I felt like a demented parrot repeating the words "We must stop and get you into dry clothes". Believe me it took all my strength to keep her from continuing that journey as she tried her best to move forward while I stripped, washed and redressed her. Lucky for me, Sarah was home from college and gathered the necessary supplies, towels, wipes, nappies, tights, knickers and so on. I quickly but gently do the best I can without upsetting or aggravating Mam. I remove her scarf, hat, coat, shoes, tights, pants and the sogging wet pad while guiding her feet onto a towel.

Once I have put her back together, wrapped up all snug and warm, I announce, "Nan we are good to go". I step out first to put the Zimmer in a position for Mam to follow but she takes one slow step forward and stops dead in her tracks. She is confused. It had taken me an age to get her to the front door only to suddenly stop the process and once again expect her to move forward. I guess the instruction to stop had now just about now registered and here we are stuck with the Zimmer on the front step. Mam was going nowhere.

The weather had turned wicked. Rain was running down my back as I had stepped out first without my coat to guide the Zimmer towards the car safely. Mam stood there, fascinated like a child experiencing wind and rain for the first time, distracted. She could not get to grips with what I needed her to do next. I am left with no choice but to bend over and gently move forward one leg after the other, each step of the way. She would take only one guided step prompted solely by the pressure of my hand on her calf and stop dead while I patiently encourage her to take another, and another, until eventually we reach the car.

When I opened the car door she dropped her head slightly, "her habit". Once again she stood, totally confused. Wild horses were not going to help make that final move into the car. I had no choice but to take her body weight and guide her on to the seat as best I could. I then quickly sat into the driving seat, baffled, knowing Mam was unaware of my struggle, unaware that I am a drowned rat, unaware that I have finally no choice but to stop these visits. It is clear that this beast Alzheimer's has once again pulled the rug out from under her feet as her brain activity is almost non-existent and her movement is now virtually impossible.

I looked at my mother sitting there bemused and could not help feeling defeated and so sad that she had been reduced to this at the end of her days. My mother had sunk deeper into another realm. Dragging her around the countryside was not going to make one bit of a difference. My heart was truly broken but like with every other stage, acceptance eventually creeps in and maybe it better pre-pared me for letting go, knowing that this was no way to live.

# A pointless charade

I found Mam this morning in her bedroom, slumped over in an armchair looking so depleted and way beyond redemption. There is no reaction to me entering her lifeless room, her little smile of acknowledgement long since gone. I help her into bed after pressing the play button on the music centre to allow a gentle tune resonate mildly in the air hoping to put some positive life back. I know there is a good chance that if Mam gets a generous hour on her back, a smidgen of spirit from the depths of her soul might reappear, and then sitting upright may not be so much of a challenge.

I open the window a little while she drifts in and out of sleep and quietly sort out her clothes, measuring to see if they need adjustment. Little do I know that her night attire is secretly lining up in the drawers beside me. I try to detach and let go, not knowing that she will shortly be confined to this bed for good. Within a few weeks she will be finished with the armchair, the wardrobe and the tired old Zimmer, sleeping mostly, her body steadily closing down.

As I quietly rearrange her wardrobe I try not to wish for a word or a peaceful feeling. All I feel is her despair and restlessness. She is missing somewhere in the Alzheimer's tunnel unable to reach us. And we can't reach her. Secretly my heart is still scrambling for a flicker of hope. But no more knowing smiles, no more tears, no more outbursts or silliness. Just desolately waiting for her maker to take her hand and beautiful soul. When she opens her eyes, that lost look of desperation has not subsided and it holds within it the ability to break the strongest of hearts.

I remember Mam praying for the end saying what a pointless charade; take me out of here. She was so right. Where is the point of all this joylessness, a spiritless body makes no sense at all no matter which way you look at it, for a loved one to be reduced to an empty shell, powerless, waiting and waiting for God to set her free. I tell you when and if I ever reach the pearly gates and if he doesn't throw me to the fires of hell first, I will have a few taxing questions for our maker.

I sit and wonder should I open the photograph albums sitting on the dresser. Or will this jog Mam's memory and make her even more distressed in her lost tunnel. Her prayers, her card playing, her recognition of people are all jumbled up. This includes the people in those photographs whom she loved and knew so well as her life line. How cruel to be stripped right back step by step, week by week, with no meaning to existence.

With as much zest as I can muster, I wheel Mam back down to the dayroom for a lunch which I know she is not going to eat. When is the right time to say enough is enough? It is so obvious there is no interest, no expression, not even wonderment or recognition. She once again sits amongst the other residents looking lifeless and blank as I lean across the table and kiss her, saying I will return soon.

Putting the best foot forward, I exit before breakdown and return to my chirpy daughters who have the ability to lift my wanting heart and put me back together to face another encounter, good or bad. These two little angels do for me what I wish I could do for my poor mother. Thank goodness at the close of day I have a guaranteed night's sleep assured, "courtesy of nursing home care" allowing my hope to float right back up to the surface with a promise attached. If only for a day that I might leave the nursing home with a heart tinged with gladness. One wishful day at a time.

> *"Perseverance is not a long race – it is many short races one after the other"* – Walter Elliot.

# Up

In the film UP, thousands of balloons lifted Carl's house right up into the air to take him on adventures. Carl was an elderly man and had planned to see the world after retirement with his wife. Unfortunately, Ellie died suddenly leaving Carl alone and lost. Carl was the image of my Dad. We got a kick out of watching this movie many times after he passed. A simple balloon can create so much joy and fun. I guarantee you the movie UP will also bring a smile or two to any family caring for a relative with Alzheimer's.

On this particular day I had to beg Lailah to pay a short visit to check in on Mam. Lailah was fed up of nursing home visits. Who could blame her as there is very seldom any reaction, shape, make or form at this stage? I am in no doubt that on entering the dayroom we will find Mam tired as the nurse has informed me she has been to the resident hairdresser. This is remarkable considering the Palliative Care Team have been called in. The medical staff have an idea that Mam's time is limited. Considering she is neither eating nor drinking, for Mam to pay a visit to the hairdresser at this stage would be the equivalent of going to the bog and taking home a load of turf single-handed with an ass and cart.

There are approximately twenty residents sitting near the entrance of the dayroom playing bingo. One of the activity leaders points to a table in the distance and there she sits alone, quietly resisting exhaustion. Yes, this day has surely knocked Mam for six. Tears slide gently down her cheeks the moment she sets eyes on us. We take her to her bedroom hoping that a rest might revive her a bit.

As I settle Mam for her rest, Lailah sits on the armchair with a pump holding a blue balloon on the end of its air funnel. This one has been pumped many times. She keeps letting the balloon slip off the funnel. With great determination and perseverance, at last she succeeds, blowing it up to its capacity and she is delighted with herself. But suddenly, once again she loses her grip on the mouth of the balloon. It slips through her fingers and flutters in circles around Mam's head tickling her nose. What a sight. Mam is suddenly alert and there is a look of surprise on her face. Her reappearance is so funny that you couldn't help but laugh.

Now, thank goodness there are tears of joy as Mam is flipped right out of her dark world and drawn into our laughter. This little woman, up to this point staring into space, worn to a thread, comes alive. Mam put her hand up suddenly wondering what was tickling her nose and started to smile. Then she began lifting her arms gently to try catching the balloons as they fluttered by. Lailah, so delighted to see her nanny uplifted, continued to blow up the remainder of the balloons with renewed enthusiasm, deliberately letting them whizz around the room. It was like watching an animation movie. We were in hysterics. Little had we known that there would be a surprise opening for fun and laughter. A delightful memory to counterbalance some of the heartbreaking ones.

I asked Lailah to write her account of that day. Here's her story, neither prompted nor edited, at the age of nine.

Written by Lailah Ellen Carty Joyce

*Today we are going in to see Nanny. We bought some balloons and a pump. It is nearly christmas eve. So we went into the Nursing Day Room. She was not having great fun at all. It's just not Nanny's day, I can tell you. So we brought Nanny down to her room and I started to pump up some balloons. Mammy started to sing a song, usually Nanny sings the next line. It certainly is not going to happen this time in my head. My balloon did not really work out that well. I tried another one. It busted and went around and around, buzzing like this, buzzzzzzzzzzzzzzzz weeeeeee. So I tried to catch it because I thought Nanny would go ballistic. But the minute I started to catch the balloon she bursted out laughing, I did too and so did mammy.*
*The end.*

# A big decision

The decision has been made. Mam will stay in the nursing home for Christmas Day and yes, probably for the remainder of her life. I know she is in good care, medical staff at hand, time allocated to personal care, feeding, bathing, dressing, and familiar bedtime schedules. God only knows these routines, although necessary, must seem at times so frigging dull and monotonous for Alzheimer's patients.

I am searching for a better word or description here. The images flickering in my over active imagination are of cows following the path each day to the milking parlour or sheep being rounded up by the farmer to be sheared. At least in the animal kingdom there must be a feeling of freedom attached to re-entering green fields, where they might run, gallop and graze at will.

Because Mam's cognitive function has little or no spark left, it seems to the entire world that these repetitive practices to all intents or purposes appear joyless. One can tell by other residents who are fully *compos mentis* that these structures and gatherings, whether for care, meals or recreational activities, are a reason to look forward. They know that they always have a choice to stay and socialise or return to their caves to knit, crochet, read, phone a friend or simply rest if they wish.

I should be over the moon that Mam will be comfortable and well looked after over Christmas. The decision has been made on concrete grounds as movement outside the home is now an ordeal for her. However, insistent doubts still manage to creep in and out, again and again. Oh God, have we made a rash decision? Maybe on this Christmas Day Mam will be in a better place and well able with a little encouragement and patience to be with family for just one more gathering. Wishful thinking. I'm afraid a clear rational decision has been made just like every other one along this gruesome road. It's time to step back and allow acceptance once more to open its doors.

My sisters spent Christmas morning with Mam in the nursing home. Thank goodness they came away happy. They found Mam content to be immersed among the festivities. That evening I also found Mam in a wonderful mood. Amazingly, she smiled, held my hand and blessed herself several times the moment she set eyes on me. We were drawn to her bedroom and as I helped her out of the wheelchair she lost balance falling into my arms while still holding that gentle smile. We swayed a little for a moment or two to the sound of Christmas music. Absolutely magical. Then, out of the blue, she was suddenly pulled in another direction. That happy feeling fell away swiftly and now Mam was rigidly standing upright like a statue looking through me as if I was a stranger.

I guess something within flicked that well-worn switch and confusion once again fell right across her face. No matter how hard I tried to encourage her to take the next step toward the bed it was as if she was rooted to the floor. Was she actually waiting in the dayroom for one of us to appear and take her out to be with family? I don't know but the pause button had certainly been tapped. I had no choice but to call for help and while I stepped aside allow the staff to assist.

I bet you are wondering if realisation had dawned at last – has Mam now well and truly tuned into nursing home care. Hindsight once again makes its logical appearance. I understand that visual images trigger Mam's next move, such as staff in uniform entering the room at a particular time, addressing her, sliding open the drawer to take out her night clothes, pulling the blinds, turning back the bed clothes, removing her teeth, etc. Is it possible that all of this commotion and conditioning sets the stage to move forward and work with the staff? Maybe this scene has become Mam's new normal. At last the nursing home has become a new abode and has an extended family. When I re-entered the room she looked as if she had seen me for the first time and smiled gently. A welcome gift as I lay down beside her and gave her a warm hug. Not such a bad Christmas Day then, after all.

I am in total awe of nursing home care right now. It is an unexpected reminder of why the decision that visits outside had to come to a natural end. Even with this condition, Mam may just have found a little comfort in the familiar. I guess the smells, the sounds, the staff, and even those dark red uniforms, which I thought were too harsh originally, now play an important part. As I type, the ringing of the Angelus bell has triggered a very old memory. In my mind's eye I can see my mother in her kitchen coming to a complete stop at the sound of this bell many years ago, a gracious lady pausing to give thanks. I guess it's true that rituals and routines draw from our memory a reason to move forward or maybe to just take a moment or two to appreciate our many blessings.

The very next day, St. Stephen's Day, was different. When Geraldine's phone began to vibrate, we knew instinctively that Sarah and Evelyn were in a quandary. They found Mam weeping desolately in the dayroom. They were taken aback. They were shocked to find Mam inconsolable and almost beyond reviving. Mam was utterly exhausted. She most needed rest and plenty of tender loving care. Christmas Day and the nursing home celebrations had clearly knocked the stuffing right out of her. It was pushing the boat out to expect flying form two days in a row. We were truly grateful for all small mercies.

# Pillar of salt

There is a story in the Bible where Lot's wife was told not to look back or she would be turned into a pillar of salt. I also know exactly what I will get as I look back. I am either a slow learner or I have a never ending supply of hope in my heart. I tell myself time and time again while leaving Mam's bedroom in the nursing home not to look back. But I do look back, day after day, wanting and wishing for a smile, a knowing look of "go on gal, you can leave me now, I'm at peace". But no. Her piercing eyes look in my direction, reaching into my heart and squeezing it until it hurts so badly. My interpretation of what she is attempting to say is, "Please don't abandon me".

The plate of liquidized food is in front of her and a care assistant has gone to find a small spoon, hoping to get a few morsels of food past Mam's lips or, with any luck, some thickened water. Each lift of that spoon will have a plea attached, willing Mam's mouth to open. It will be a game of patience, encouragement and perseverance on the care assistant's part.

I wish with all my heart it could still be me helping her but she has now become accustomed to certain members of staff and sometimes she will accommodate them. Not that she wants anything at this stage; she is well fed with enough food and water. We all have tried in vain. Even Geraldine has stopped buying the little jelly trifles which used to lift Mam's spirit at bedtime. Over the past few months Mam is declining further and I think even if she wanted, her brain would not send a message to the muscles to open her mouth. It is such a ridiculous condition.

To have faith and move forward. To not continuously look back and let this condition consume me. To stop scratching for the homely feeling I once had with her in the past and to be at home within myself. Looking back, if I had been this wise, the reflection of my light alone might have been enough to diminish her unease. It might be enough to know that this was an impasse, maybe not such a pleasant one but nevertheless, a transition beyond comprehension, a step in letting go and letting God handle the details.

Shining a light for another human being is the greatest gift of all. I knew without a doubt that there were times even amongst others she was lost at sea. It was not about me leaving her stranded. It was about accepting the darkness as a part of her world and reminding myself if I were to dig deep enough there were times I helped shine a light on the obscurity of the Alzheimer's world. But these hours, minutes and moments happened when I was not looking for anything in return, when I did not need Mam to reappear after shaking off this monster.

I still felt at times that I could have done much more if acceptance had arrived at my door earlier but hindsight is a wonderful thing. You just do not get it until you get it. It is easy to look back but as hard as hell to look forward and grab that wisdom before it is too late to administer the gift of our own light. I now know that it is our job to do our best with the information at hand and grow into our shoes as we go along. But the persistent want to erase all moments of darkness, that look of desperation, can cloud what we already have to offer even if it is just to hold the hand or heart of a lost soul for a moment or two.

# Death by chocolate

Angels take themselves lightly. As I drove warily towards the nursing home I noticed my sister, Evelyn, ahead. Was I happy to see that car? I slammed my fist on the horn, flashed the head lights, and waved out the window like a lunatic, hoping to get her attention. She was much too engrossed listening to a match on the radio, obviously paying little attention to her rear view mirror. My eager heart did an almighty jig as she indicated left while approaching the slip road to the nursing home.

A sigh of relief escapes me. What a blessing to have a larger-than-life family to bounce off, as some of these visits were more than taxing. Better chance of drawing a smile out of me Mam today.

We pulled into the nursing home parking area, one behind the other, knowing full well our only mission now was to lift the atmosphere in Mam's room and leave knowing that we were of some benefit. Wishful thinking. There was not a flicker of recognition from Mam when we entered the room. She was like a little lost lamb, her piercing eyes looking beyond us with wonderment. The food charts tell that Mam is eating and drinking little, except a spoonful of this or that every few hours. We try also to feed her to no avail. It's no wonder Mam's body is gradually withdrawing into the mattress, vanishing further more and more each day.

Evelyn, my sister, the baby of the family, now in her early forties, has the ability to make a cat laugh, or on the other hand, to make a grown man cry. She is some character. Sometimes one might wonder did she fall off the conveyer belt and into a different mould when God was dispatching the Joyce clan. Da was the boss of our household until Evelyn came along. Then he got a rude awakening. When she was old enough to change the channels on the TV, me Da reluctantly had to take a back seat. Evelyn was a force to be reckoned with. It was Tom and Jerry or the highway. No one else had the balls to cross him. We used to sit there waiting for him to explode but his only retaliation was to turn on his heels, spew a litany of abuse and leave the room, slamming the door for better effect. Evelyn won every time.

If anyone was going to bring a smile to Mam's face, it was our Evelyn. When she had a mission to accomplish, there would be no stone left unturned. The packet of chocolate buttons on the dressing table was the first port of call. The girls in our family are serial chocoholics. For every occasion and every mood swing, a swift drive to a local sweet counter is in order. This failing causes a swifter trip to a beer counter.

Mam accepted the first chocolate button but unfortunately it had no positive effect. She still lay there motionless staring into space. Evelyn gave me one of her massive smiles and a wink, meaning don't give up girl. I leaned over the bed once again and was just about to give Mam a second one when a nurse entered the room and caught me in action. I sat back as quick as lightning, shoved the packet of chocolate buttons under the quilt like a bold child up to mischief and laughed. I know you are probably wondering why hide the treats but few people have the same regard for the choc drug as we do. This nurse I guess was no fool. Maybe the chocolate on Mam's lips was the give-away as she immediately pointed to the head of the bed, indicating that a more upright position while feeding or drinking might be more appropriate.

Evelyn, having sizeable experience in the computerised world had no problem changing the position of the mechanical bed, placing Mam in a perfect position. If it were left up to me, lacking in technology skills, Mam and the bag of buttons might have been sandwiched into that mattress, which would have whipped up a completely different story. You will never believe what happened next. Moments after receiving another chocolate button, Mam started to choke. Holy shit, the atmosphere was now destined to take a further nose dive. God love us.

Myself and Evelyn looked at each other with shock and surprise. Hadn't we done what was suggested – taken the best course of action and risen the bed? That particular expression of shock while registering between us must have been comical because instead of screaming for help or pressing the alarm button we fell into a right heap on the bed laughing. Our giddiness was so infectious that it caught Mam off guard and she too started to laugh, so much so that tears were running down her cheeks. The motion obviously cleared her throat giving her instant relief. It was a good job we were able to laugh rather than get ourselves into a real fluster, which no doubt saved both our skins for another day.

The realisation that Mam's life could have come to an abrupt end because of one Cadbury's chocolate button escalated our giddiness. Could you just imagine the headlines? I guess this adds another dimension to the term "death by chocolate". That little chocolate button, be it right or wrong, lifted all our spirits.

Of course after this episode another penny was just about to drop. It was easier to understand now why Mam's food had to be at a certain consistency to accommodate a declining swallow.

However, the giggle the three of us had was worth the drama and gave Mam a lift for a moment or two.

# Charts and more charts

Mam's food chart today reads, 'Two teaspoons of liquid, five teaspoons of dinner, refused the rest'. Day by day now, her charts read something of the same type of message. The one reaction left is Mam's hand going up into the air firmly to block food entering her mouth. When I use the word 'firmly' I mean 'with attitude'. There are no half-assed measures, she means business. There is no hope of getting food past her lips; the look on her face is enough.

I do not blame her at this stage. Her food is liquidised, drinks are thickened, and I could easily do a jig on top of the tea it is so dense. Funny, no one knows if Mam is in a state of disinterest, has no need at this stage for food or has the feeding process become so uncomfortable because of her declining swallow. It's probably all of the above.

This brings to mind what me Da used to say when I was worrying about getting food into my children as toddlers. "Leave the child alone, he will drink when he is thirsty and he'll eat when he's hungry". It would make you wonder about drip feeds and thickeners. Are we interfering with nature and the process of slowing down and letting go? Looking back it seems ludicrous. I know for sure Mam's hand shot up long before we gave up trying to feed her.

I made Mam a little more comfortable with pillows and took her hand out from under the blankets. I sat there humming songs and as I did, she gently squeezed my hand. Even these little gestures make me feel that the presence of a family member or a good friend may be crucial right now for comfort. She has that 'missing in space', 'nobody is home' expression but somehow deep down in my gut I sense a feeling of grace. I wonder sometimes, what is God waiting for. Surely he will call me Mam before she completely disappears into a skeleton under these sheets.

My Mam has a real look of her grandchildren now. Her face is getting finer, translucent, more porcelain, more like a doll, every day. She doesn't change expression or move much. But I did notice as I sang Amazing Grace earlier today that she gently tried to mouth the words. But there is no sound and no energy. Not even a chocolate button will pass those lips.

I decided yesterday that I would stop saying goodbye when I am leaving her room as she held my hand so tight as I tried to leave her bedside. All of a sudden a look of a lost frightened child came over her and tears started to come into her eyes. Does she know something? Does she feel she is nearing the end?

# The wait

Well it may be a new beginning for us but it is definitely heading somewhere towards the end for Ellen Joyce who gracefully resigned to her bed to wait for the final call.

At last it is easier now. This may sound horrible but going into the dayroom day after day recently to find Mam slumped over and drifting in and out of consciousness was soul destroying. It is an unnatural way of existing, a way of just putting up with another day, like dragging your feet. Mam will probably finish out her days in this bedroom, free from pain. It's a blessing, thank goodness, that she is drifting in and out of a restful state. Lord knows she needs to be on the flat of her back, comfortable and peaceful at last. No more pulling and dragging down the corridor to the dayroom, no more sitting waiting in a sea of despair.

Mam occasionally yawns, smiles or sheds a tear of joy or sadness. For me it's a little bit like getting high when a newborn smiles. But our wise ones are quick to inform us that it is just a bit of wind. It is hard to know, but my intuition is telling me she is finally at peace.

We are down to living in the now. At last no more questions to ask or answer. All the analysing, the research and the wondering is over. There is just the wait. Ellen Joyce is resigned to bed to wait and wait and wait, refusing food and water. She may think she can will herself out of this world but the forces that be, have their own plan. Maybe the gods are trying our patience, love, honour, dependability and resilience. They are testing a tough bunch.

Spending time at Mam's bedside now is as peaceful as it is going to get. The struggle with Alzheimer's is over. The madness has made its exit after relentlessly grinding down Mam's spirit. At last she lies gently drifting. Tranquillity has descended in room 39. We are told Mam is at the end stage. We have no idea how long we have left with her. The only concrete reaction now is the way she holds hands with the bed-sitter. There is a definite feeling that she wants company. Mam can relax. All stops have been put in place. She does not have to use her energy to slap the hand that tries to feed her anymore. This action had been given absolution at last. Mam can now receive with openness our prayers, warmth and love. At last all the lucky stars are beginning to line up and await this angel.

# The Palliative Care Team is in

It is now two years since the nursing home became my mother's new residence. The Palliative Care Team has been called in. The nursing home staff are aware that Mam's journey is coming to an end. She is fading.

According to the Alzheimer's guide notes, Mam will exit this world at the beginning and not the end of stage seven. She will mercifully be saved the discomfort of physical rigidity. Believe it or not, her good old tormentor had reached the finish line and "calm" has reappeared on many levels. It's a welcome blessing.

Her chart says "Confined to bed and refusing food or drinks". The word "refusing" is harsh as it is impossible to know what type of message if any, Mam's brain is receiving. Is she fed up of this ridiculous condition or is she naturally retreating gently hoping her weary soul will return to the sod as John O'Donohue might say. Maybe she just has no desire for food as she is not active. Yet, she still has the ability to shield her mouth from anything entering. This is still a wonder to me considering her communication barrier is well constructed. A determined hand goes up as clearly and as resolutely as a Garda stopping traffic, time and time again to cover her mouth. Tell me how this one action is still guaranteed. Amusing really.

It is yet another new beginning in our Alzheimer's story and at last a peaceful one. I am so relieved to say Mam is now confined to bed. Gone are the dark bewildering days of finding this wonderful lady slumped over in no man's land, discontented amongst the other residents.

I'm not sure if Mam is being assisted into the shower anymore or if she is having bed baths. I cannot even allow myself to think of a hoist being used. I can now walk into the nursing home with a lighter heart, confident I will find peace at large in her bedroom. Thank God, the only expected action now is for Mam to drift in and out of sleep.

Mam has weathered this storm. The struggle is over and she can now dwell in a well-deserved calm atmosphere. Stress at last has flung its hook out the window. A part of me will always wonder whether Mam's recurring emotional outbursts during the latter part of her condition related to Alzheimer's itself or just being worn down by constant central heating, lack of fluids and stimulation. But thank goodness, it is finally heart-warming to find Mam in a more restful position with her head supported, warm and clean in great care, with our beautiful Palliative Care nurse ready to alleviate any discomfort.

The one sure thing is there are no answers. Each case of Alzheimer's is completely different. One must readjust and accept each step along the way as there were countless beginnings and endings. It has been a fascinating, terrifying, heart-breaking journey with the capacity to unravel core strengths. Other members of my family might feel differently. They would have to sieve through their experience, and given their unique personalities and abilities, accept life's journey.

For some, the journey may have been a strong breeze rather than a hurricane.

# The grip

Geraldine has phoned to ask me to sit with Mam for a while. The nursing home has informed her that Mam had a very high temperature overnight and that she now seems anxious. The emotion in Geraldine's voice tells it all. Geraldine is not happy to be out of town and rarely leans towards sentimentality. We have yet again sensed a change and we are afraid to admit that Mam is telling us by her grip that she does not want to be left alone. She knows, as do we, that the end is near.

I grab my car keys and run, immersed in panic and sadness at the thoughts of Mam's aloneness or want of family at her bedside. It's funny that I constantly tell people I have poor visualisation skills. But the picture is clear. I can see Mam in her room lying on her side and deep within longing for family comfort. I have held her hand gently over the last few months hoping for a little squeeze of recognition. Sadly, there was nothing. Now there is a definite grip which tells a different story.

I enter the room and the nurse stands up gently and gives me a knowing gentle smile. I walk to Mam's bedside and lift her hand with care. There is a mad rattle from deep within her chest, her eyes are fading but telling that she is longing for comfort and company. The nurse who made the phone call to Geraldine is right. I am flipping between two states of calm and grief while wiping away the flow of tears as they run down my cheeks, praying to God to take her now and spare her any further bodily breakdown.

While looking into my eyes I know she knows the content of my prayers and gently in my mind I tell her I love her and she must not be afraid to let go if the time is right. She has a vice-like grip for the duration of each cough which reminds me of labour pains. I don't know if she is actually in pain or if the vibration is causing her distress.

While holding my hand, there is a non-verbal conversation – "I am frightened, please stay with me". I think the sensation and sound of that cough is making her reach out and the nurse suggests the same. Mam now needs reassurance. There must be someone watching over her at all times now.

To lighten the situation the nurse says with a smile that the decorators have been in and yes, it is amazing what the staff have done with the room. It is heavenly. Mam gradually drifts off to sleep after a blessing from Father Noonan. There is gentle piano music in the background, vases of flowers everywhere, Da's photo on the dresser and the hum of the fan keeping her temperature down. I am wrapped up in a blanket as the nurse returns with a tray of food. She places it quietly on a table beside me. I have no interest and it would feel wrong to eat now.

Valerie has entered the room quietly to let me know that Palliative Care have been called and they are discussing 'putting on a pump'. I can't take it in. The atmosphere has changed. It feels so graceful and calm. Absolute respect has descended. Every sound and moment is now precious and accounted for. I feel blessed and in the presence of angels. I think each staff member has been handpicked at this time by the Lord. They are the ones Mam would have been proud to have at her bedside to also say goodbye in silent prayers of comfort.

# The final call

At 10.30 p. m. on Sunday 24th February 2013, the nursing home informed us that Mam was nearing the end. Funny how time suddenly stands still. It's like being in a vacuum. There is nothing more important in the world. Everything else fades into the background. Our only mission was to get to the nursing home.

I remember an emotional stillness descending on me while driving the car for the last time in my Mam's direction. The reachable members of our family sat at Mam's bedside for the final hours and at five minutes to one on February 25th 2013, Ellen Carty Joyce's soul departed this earth and ascended straight to Heaven. Of this I have no doubt.

For two and a half hours we sat and listened to Mam's rhythmic breath, never laboured. Even as we chatted quietly, it was faintly noticeable like a clock ticking gently in the background. I am recalling from my meditation book a description of the breath as an anchor. Mam's anchor was just about to be raised allowing her spirit set sail to glory in Paradise.

Her breaths gradually became shallow, closer together and eventually no more as her inner clock gently stopped ticking. Even though expected, it was hard to believe. This transition was so stress-free and acceptable. No other action or reaction, no cough, no sigh or change was noticeable except that her eyes suddenly told a deeper story – that "Ellen Joyce no longer resides in this vessel".

They say that if you look intently into someone's eyes you can see their soul. That's exactly how it felt. A door had gently, yet undeniably, closed and what was left of Mam's spirit had departed in a graceful, no-fuss way, leaving behind a room charged with emotion, relief, peace, grace, acceptance, wonder and loss. Little did we know that plenty of it was patiently waiting around each and every corner for us. I recall Geraldine saying that how Mam passed away was testament to the way she lived; calmly and quietly, true to her natural spirit, like a gentle breeze passing in the night. It is fascinating how we go about our daily lives so far removed from the presence of our spirit and unaware of the importance of our breath.

From the time I received the phone call to get to Mam's bedside I felt drawn toward something wonderful. It is inexplicable. Maybe it was the fact that I knew I was going to be immersed in a sea of love and care, surrounded by family who all had the same wish – for Mam to pass gracefully and with comfort. That wish was granted with much more loveliness than one could ever imagine. For this blessing we will be forever grateful.

The immediate reaction was unimaginable emptiness. Even now if I were to say the words, "God bless Mam", I go back to the moment and the feeling of the cord being cut. We were all now chucked out in the cold to walk alone, stripped of all parental influence. We had no choice but to move forward now, knowing full well our mother was no longer reachable in physical form but the memory of those final calm breaths still lingered warm and palpable.

The staff members in the nursing home that night were Heaven-sent. We left the room to give them time to prepare Mam for the final step of her journey and reorganise the room. When we re-entered the room, it was like Mam had magically gone back in time and the strain of the last few years had lifted. Our easy acceptance of this wondrous transition lay in the knowledge that our mother was now free from the torture of Alzheimer's.

This ease was heightened by the nursing home support team members. Their vigilance and sense of knowingness of end of life timing was so accurate it amazed us. Their care, compassion and wisdom was a gift from God for Mam and for us. We felt totally supported with grace. This gave us time to prepare and dwell in those final moments with love and comfort and a deep, deep sense that all would be taken care of, giving us the opportunity to be a part of this final journey with Mam and to gradually move forward with another serene memory of a gathering of agreeable easy hearts.

# The wake

It was not planned although the gods may have had some influence. I know I suggested my house moments after Mam passed but I had not a clue what it might entail except I was sure that leaving Mam in "The House of Rest" was going to break my heart. It just seemed fitting as Mam had spent many afternoons resting on my bed over the past few years. The troops rallied around, coming and going, cleaning, manoeuvring, moving and dismantling until we were left with a scene fit for an angel. Thanks to Sarah and John no stone was left unturned. We could safely call my sister Sarah, "The Queen of Clean". Thank God there is one in every family.

I remember secretly peeping out the bathroom door. Sarah was cleaning in areas that had not seen a mop in many years while I happily painted the bathroom wall which had been screaming out for attention. It was like having those people in from those shows on TV with eight hours to revamp a home.

Mam would have been impressed although someone put my Valentine lilies outside the back door because they didn't particularly like the scent. To tell the truth they were probably well past their sell-by date and clearly had started to smell like dirty old socks. I am guessing it was our Geraldine because she is the only one daring enough. She does things on impulse. If it were me, in her house, I would be like a female version of Mr Bean making a "Will I? Won't I?" decision.

Someone else took the bedroom door down, but was not so quick to put it back up. I won't mention "John Joyce". The nuts and bolts of my bed disappeared too. Only last week when I moved the bed to Hoover under it, I noticed two nuts were missing as the bed almost fell apart. Me Mam must have been holding it up.

Uncle Anthony, Mam's younger brother, got right behind us for the wake and dealt with stuff that would never have crossed our minds, like traffic control. I did not realise there was a tradition where the mourners spray holy water with a twig or a little branch of a palm tree over the corpse. Who else would think about these things? The rest of my family were busy making decisions and necessary arrangements for the funeral. Whatever was needed Anthony managed to pull out of a hat. He produced large water heaters for making endless cups of tea. He produced the utensils and brass candle holders that were real official ones similar to those in the church. He moved around us with great care and patience helping it come together perfectly.

I felt no stress or anxiety as we waited for the hearse to arrive. Once again a gentle calm descended. It felt no different from waiting for the final home visits when Mam was then only physically present.

I secretly wished that Mam would look good in the coffin, simply to not frighten Lailah or anyone else for that matter. It can be soul-destroying to see a corpse if their features have dramatically changed and are no more than a shadow of their former self. Many times in the final few weeks I got a fright when entering Mam's room in the nursing home as she was gradually disappearing in the bed, looking vacant and tormented, her body shrinking right before our eyes. I knew that people who had not seen her on a regular basis were sure to be shocked at the change in her appearance.

Mam arrived in the hearse at four o'clock in the afternoon. When we entered the bedroom after the funeral director had left, it was an enchanting scene. There was a sense of wonderment and godliness. It was as if the angels had descended spraying the air with serenity making the time left precious as we got to say our goodbyes without fuss or haste. Mam looked really wonderful in the coffin, the strain was gone and the reflection of the pink satin interior enhanced her complexion.

One by one, the entire world came to pay their respects. I mean the entire world. Mam did not stand out from the crowd and make her presence known, being quiet and gentle in nature. I was not expecting this never-ending flow of people. If only my mother knew how highly respected she was. These people moved gracefully through our house.

I remember my brother, John, calling me earlier that day, saying that Elaine was on her way to help. There I was thinking "help with what?" Boy, was all this support needed! I had no clue of the number of friends Mam had. Never ever had my mother spoken about her association with others. I could not see her having all those followers. They were like her – quiet, calm and spiritual.

After we had all left the nest, Mam found her wings and learned to drive in order to pick up the boss from the pub but then she got drawn into the world of gambling.

She toured the countryside alongside other loyal card sharks who had a precious few euro to squander. I remember Geraldine telling me that Mam would never allow the stakes to be raised in order to give everyone a chance, rich or poor. She never got cross. She just ensured that gentle look of wisdom, "Let's keep this simple". No matter who won the miniscule pot, she was always more than delighted for them. I guess it was during these excursions that her sweetness was gathered honourably by other upright citizens.

At one stage there was a lull as a half dozen sympathisers sat quietly with Mam. I suggested a decade of the Rosary while Geraldine was in the room. She held the Catholic faith close to her heart. One out of eleven is not bad. Our Geraldine is programmed to sit, stand, genuflect and say the right thing at the right time. It is important to have at least one of these in a family. But then, to my horror, the priest called Geraldine out of the room. I was left to lead the Rosary. I floundered in an expectant silence. I could not remember. Thankfully, a compassionate neighbour put me out of my misery and started the ball rolling again by revisiting the same decade.

I stood sheepishly begging the Lord above for mercy telling him with conviction that I would get my act together if he would send Geraldine back in to finish the job properly. Did I honour my word? Not at all. I still only know the Our Father and Hail Mary.

There was no end to the trays of food, wonderful lasagne and cups of tea appearing out of thin air. There was no end to the laughter, tears, stories, prayers. Yes, there had been plenty of need for all the help. I'm sure John was well and truly amused with me. I had not a clue. All of these sympathisers arrived one by one because somewhere in their hearts they held memories of this quiet, graceful lady and needed to say farewell. Maybe some had never met Mam but they knew she was a great spirit because they had encountered one of us eleven or me wild, straight-up and honourable Da.

# The funeral

The little church on the hill was where me Mam walked us to Mass without fail every Sunday and Holy Day during our childhood.

I woke up beside Lailah on the crisp morning of the funeral, 27th February 2013. I could not bring myself to sleep alone. We were comfort for each other. I remember being surprised that even during my sleep state I was at a loss for me Mam as both my cheeks and the pillow were damp. An unsettling feeling of sadness hit me at this realisation and it took all I had to hold back the sobs for fear of waking the little bundle sleeping peacefully beside me.

Lailah felt my despair. She looked up at me and said, "Are you sad about Nanny, Mam?" I felt numb, like a great big hole had been exposed in my chest leaving my heart vulnerable and raw. There was neither wind nor energy left in this balloon but the compassionate look on the child's face was enough to lift me to face the day ahead.

"The Removal" had taken place the night before. This was the movement by the funeral director of the coffin from the family home to the little church on the hill. What an impact this word "removal" had on me. It felt like a word you might associate with a piece of furniture. Logically, I knew Mam was going to be placed in the earth on the following day but

I could not get to grips with an overnight stay in a dark, cold church.

By the time the doorbell rang for the first time we were beginning to feel lighter. One by one my sisters arrived. Funny, it felt a bit like getting ready for a family wedding. There was a right old mixture of emotions at play in my kitchen. It was like stepping out of your body and looking at a movie. We were all actors and we were in a rehearsal for a play, each one of us having our own parts to play in this farewell. All we needed was a director. The gatherings in my kitchen up to this point had been about care for Mam. A new journey was about to start. One door was closing and another opening. The road forward now was without its original directors. No wonder it felt unreal. It was.

There we were, all seated in the little church on the hill to celebrate our mother's life and to let go gracefully. The church was packed to capacity. People came out of the woodwork, left, right and centre. Each handshake, each tear, each expression was filled with sweet memories and that heart-warming connection. It was communication through expression. My mother's quiet disposition had drawn all these like-minded people to pay their respects.

It was easy to tell that these mourners were her people, people who led quiet, worthy lives shielding their care and paying little attention to the expanding world of materialism. I believed my Mam to have been an "ordinary" little lady who had the gift of minding her own business. This word evolved to "extraordinary" over those few days and the weeks that followed.

There were mystical waves of calm and peace, laughter and tears as different members of the family moved through the readings and participated in the ceremony. My brothers and sisters were overwhelmed as tears of loss and love dripped down their cheeks. They were moved by displays of admiration as sweet memories of my mother's life flooded their consciousness.

Geraldine wrote and read the following poem at the end of the service before we walked Mam to her new resting place and watched as she was lowered into the earth while the notes of The Lonesome Boatman drifted soulfully through the air.

*Mam*

*Born in the Island 82 years ago,*
*an angel from Heaven was sent here to glow.*
*Mike was the love of her long happy life,*
*she was loving and giving, the world's perfect wife.*
*Reared 11 of us, 7 girls and 4 boys,*
*No wonder her bladder was close to her eyes.*

*Went to Mass and said prayers every spare minute,*
*we were blessed and protected by every saint in it.*
*She played cards like a shark, this is well known,*
*read books by the hundred, it kept her going.*

*Her kindness to others, it's fair to be said,*
*was known to us all, like her lovely brown bread.*

*A great friend and mother we all hold so dear,*
*will be missed by us daily but still will be near.*
*For Heaven awaits such a beautiful one,*
*she'll watch over us there as she's always done.*

– Geraldine Joyce

A community of hearts surrounded Mam's graveside to release her to the heavens knowing that me Da was waiting with outstretched arms at the end of this long and well-lived journey. The story of Ellen and Mike Joyce began once again, now in our hearts, spirits and memories.

There were moments I remember feeling like someone had taken my heart out and had squeezed the last bit of spirit out of it leaving me wondering if life would ever be the same again.

The days turned into weeks and as we got back to reality the emptiness started to be filled up with other stuff such as remembering to put the bins out and getting Lailah back to school. Then one day I found myself humming a song, thinking happy thoughts and I realised I had started to naturally move forward.

# Hello grief

An unexpected little visitor came today. I took Lailah, now aged seven, back to school. She had a full week off following Mam's funeral as she developed a throat infection, barking cough, and a very high temperature. She was miserable as was I with no sleep for a week. Out of somewhere we got the strength to get through Mam's passing, wake, and funeral without an emotional breakdown. There were just moments of sadness accompanied by tears. I told myself that the last few years of adjusting and readjusting to each stage of Alzheimer's had prepared us for letting go, long before Mam's departure. For God's sake, how many times did I fall to the ground during this period and sob over Mam's gradual disappearance and loss of senses. Was this not enough?

Lailah got up and dressed for school. We couldn't find her running shoes. She did not like the way I presented her cornflakes and she would not take her medication. She looked like death warmed up and I wondered should I give her more time. We walked around to the school, late. Both our hearts were in our shoes and our feet dragging the ground. In my head I am saying, 'Focus on the positive', and the teacher will call if Lailah is not ready yet to be back in the classroom. I had written a note explaining her absence from school and that I am two minutes away if she feels unwell.

I turned towards the office to give a member of staff the note when Catherine and Fiona spot me and indicate for me to enter the office. All I want to do is run. I feel the flood gates open and start to curse myself for not taking another day out, wondering why this is happening right now. Could it not have stalled until I returned home? But the pain rises from deep in my chest to my throat and I cannot speak as these massive tears start to sprout from my tired eyes. Catherine takes Lailah by the hand and off to class while Fiona sits me in the office and consoles me. I am looking at her, thinking, 'Jesus, this lady really has a wonderful gift'. She then takes my hands gently and allows me to cry. I feel truly blessed to be supported by these angels.

Fiona tells me that I am the lucky one with the ability to let go and express this massive loss. I feel about six years old, abandoned, lost, not wanting to move forward, and rooted to the office chair. I so want to crawl under a quilt in my mother's care with the smell of home-cooking in the background, to be lulled into a world of contentment and security. Ridiculous really, considering I had not slept like this since my childhood home well over thirty years ago. It's the beauty of grief I guess. I thought that Alzheimer's had killed off all those memories. Instead, they were ready and waiting to be acknowledged once more.

Miss Corbet enters the office and reassures me that she will keep a good eye on Lailah. She also informs me about Lailah's infection, saying that a bunch of her students including her own 10-year-old child has been subjected to it and saying it is a hard one to shift. Although this is truly reassuring, the tears continue to flow and there is not a thought running through my mind at this point, just raw emotion. I leave the office and hide under my scarf all the way home, sobbing.

Even though I am crying right now I also feel a calming essence restoring my heart as I touch each key. As wondrous as it was for grief to grip me at this time in this way, I am equally surprised that a warming sensation has gently found its way back into my blood stream and is lifting my spirit.

The time to grieve is different for each of us. Some may be able to keep it under their hats, but I have been surprised again and again at its appearance out of nowhere and how it presents itself without caution or consideration. It comes clean out of the blue. Sometimes when we think we are ready to move forward, there is a different plan in store.

I loved Mam to bits, and I know now that every unplanned episode of grief is recognition of her importance in our world as a mother. I also know she is worthy of each and every tear and feeling of loss. I know that before long these episodes will be no more and that this will be another part of letting Mam go in spirit also.

What would we be otherwise? Empty shells, robots moving from one meaningless situation to another without regard or empathy, without ever being thrown to the earth with grief or uplifted to the stars with joy and elation. A wise old Buddha said once upon a time in a far off distant land: "One must be prepared with open hearts to receive each and every emotional visitor with respect, love and compassion."

# Grief revisited

Here we go again. I am minding my own business, getting on with life, worrying about the small stuff and wham, out of the blue something blasts right through me like a tornado.

I was on the road to the NCT centre in Tullamore, my local town, to have my car tested for road worthiness. As usual, pushing time, wondering if I would actually make the appointment, I was hoping there would be someone at the car wash to make it presentable. I was attending a training course at this time and the only other thing on my mind was letting my study partner down later as I had missed the previous class due to Mam's funeral.

I can promise you the loss of Mam was far from my mind. Out of nowhere a pain gripped me in my chest. It was like someone shot right into my heart from over the graveyard wall. I did not even see the church because of all the other stuff on my mind. It was like driving to a city and missing all the villages on the way because you are rummaging through a barrage of shit to be sorted before day's end. It seemed like an eternity of gripping pain in my chest.

I guess Mam saw me speeding past the graveyard with not so much as a prayer or a glance in her direction and decided a wake-up call was in order. I was not going to be let move on that quickly only a few short breaths after her funeral. Who did I think I was codding. It felt like someone had a vice grip on my throat, as great big fat tears tumbled down my face. There is no reasoning with grief.

As I neared the car wash, I prayed to regain some degree of control. I now had a wonderful vision of me sobbing in the garage and having to write my request on damp paper for the attendant. I rooted in my bag for a pen and pad and while doing so, as suddenly as the grief had hit, it was replaced with a wave of calm. A miracle. For the first time in my life, my prayers were answered before turning grey. I felt wiped out. But there was also a sense of relief as I sat in that car sorting my study notes for a class later. I was able to focus on the small stuff once again.

In the NCT centre a lady who knew my mother reached out to sympathise with me. Little did she know I had just had a swift visit from the department of woe. We sat and conversed while she told many stories about her encounters with Mam. Less than a half hour beforehand I was a weeping mess.

The car passed the test. That evening my study partner took my hand and told me he was a grief counsellor. If feelings surfaced during any class, he was on board. I was just overwhelmed by the generosity of human spirit and began to wonder if there was an angel around every corner. Although I appreciated his gesture and good nature, I did not have to lean on him as Mam was by now caught up in the dazzling lights of Heaven. Or so I thought. Those episodes of gripping emotion eventually dissolved and led to a reinforced connection with the wonder of life. I had so many plans that day, but nature has its own aim, way beyond my control. As we make plans, God has a right old laugh.

# Nelly the second

You would not know by our Mike where the little puppy came from. It may have been a gift, a stray, a done deal or a brown envelope job. Nevertheless, this cute little thing arrived in his care.

Being a serious dude, Mike started to tick the boxes. He brought Nelly to the vet for the necessary check-up, injections, chips and worm dose. How I love that word "dose". It's probably what Mike called me after my Psych Doc interview some sixteen months earlier. We have all been called a dose by someone at one stage or another in our lives. Our Mike is approximately six foot tall, slim build, and some might just say handsome.  Well, off he trots to the vets, a skip in his step with his new little treasure, a beautiful little puppy, a diversion, a new energy, a possible gun dog.

Hard to believe what happens next. The vet calls this six foot tall lad with the ball of fluff into the surgery. After pleasantries the vet opens a new file and the serious business of the puppy begins.

The vet does not realise that the next simple question will be so detrimental. "What is the name of this new pup, Mike?" My brother goes to open his gob but is surprisingly dumb as he feels unbidden tears spring to his eyes without consideration. Jesus, Mary and Joseph, not tears. Not now. He grabs the pup and runs for his life to the car crying uncontrollably. It dawns on him. He cannot answer the vet's question because Nelly is his Mam's name.

It is Mike's  time to feel the loss of the mother who worshipped the ground he walked, her favourite son, or so he was killed telling her. You see grief does not warn you not to leave your house in case you make a complete show of yourself. It has absolutely no mercy. It was my brother's turn to feel strong emotion, a separation, a cutting of the cord. He thought all he had to do was buy a fluffy puppy and call it Nelly in order to replace me Mam.

Perhaps God was up there in the heavens this particular day, pressing sorrowful buttons, his aim, six foot men with fluffy pets who have lost a significant other, needing a sharp wake-up call. I still have this vision of the little fur ball trying to shake herself dry as tears drip from my brother's cheeks as he makes a beeline for the car. What a wonderful scene.

I am glad Mike Joyce is human. He has since given up shooting and Nelly is now a beautiful fully grown dog who, just like me Mam, is much too sensitive to chase rabbits or pheasants.

# Why did my Mam get Alzheimer's?

Sometimes I wonder what this condition Alzheimer's is all about. Does it only affect the calm little souls, the ones who have journeyed through a life time unruffled and seemingly accepting of each gruelling mountain climb? In my eyes Mam was just like this. I would take a problem to her table and the cure was always a cup of tea and an assurance, "This, too, shall pass."

I was not blessed with her wonderful disposition and I often pondered if, in fact, I have a disproportionate amount of Joyce blood in my veins. Mam's family honestly must have arisen from a gene pool of peace and quiet. Anyway, does Alzheimer's land on these seemingly calm souls in later life to allow unexpressed anger its day and with it the opportunity to say "Oh Shit" instead of "Oh Sugar". Does it allow them to be silly and playful, or to simply jump off the fence an odd time and have a strong opinion right or wrong?

Or I wonder in Mam's case if she needed to switch off because she was worn down by a life of repeated tasks caring for eleven children and attending to me Da's every need. I still have this picture of me Da hobbling out to the kitchen months before he died to give his account of "Judge Judy" and request a glass of orange juice, which he would simply get himself if Mam was out. Mam continuously gave from her heart. Nothing ever looked like a chore. Each request was responded to with ease and gentleness.

Or is there an unfathomable reason some must get close to the finish line without completing the circle of life and return to childhood before departing, and then immediately re-enter and get another chance? Is my Mam out there in a cosy baby basket ready to start again? Is it possible that someone will get to set the table for her this time around?

It is a given that a percentage of the human race is bound to know someone who will have to face this journey just like we have. If it's not personally, then it will be a close family member or a relative. It may hit like cancer or any other undesirable condition.

Was it triggered as result of Da's sudden death? Wasn't he the great love of Mam's life, her rock and motivator, the other half of her existence and a very necessary link to her well-being? They were old-school types of unexpressed love. It was not easy to see one of them without the other. Their worlds may not have been operational.

Imagine I thought that Mam would have welcomed a break after a good fifty years from steeping Da's porridge at night, setting the table for breakfast and listening to his account of every other TV show. After his retirement, Da got into a fine routine of doing his chores, having many cat naps and re-porting everything to Mam from the weather to every bit of world news he picked up in the newspapers or the TV. Do some of us need another to function properly? If so, I find it sweet that they met and had a journey together. Setting that table each night may have been as important as each breath she drew.

I don't know if there are "answers". Maybe the key to everything arduous in life is learning the art of acceptance. All I know for sure is that Mam started showing signs directly after receiving the news of Da's sudden death. Or had we missed something before that? Was it hiding in the background from the time she was diagnosed with cancer a few years earlier? That could have been the shock that started the ball rolling.

Maybe as the saying goes, all through her child-rearing years my graceful Mam was actually the proverbial duck gliding across calm waters seemingly content with its little webbed feet thrashing underneath the surface. I wonder had life itself taken its toll.

Or maybe, Alzheimer's was one final gift from Mam that dragged us together kicking and screaming for her care and maybe as a bonus to see our own strengths and weaknesses.

Maybe its purpose was to build a new foundation for us to move forward upon. Maybe it was family, a link to our past and a bridge to our future.

# The value of a good hug

I spent my childhood, if not my entire life, wanting to see some gesture of affection between my parents. There were no hugs and kisses in our home but somehow in the later years there was a knowingness attached to an elusive feeling that maybe, just maybe, they loved each other in their own reserved way. If you were aware enough, there was always that loving smile when there was a bit of banter going on. Imagine they got up each morning without fail to tend to us until we left the nest as straight up citizens. Shouldn't this have been enough? Did I need the gesture of affection, the odd bear hug or pat on the back now and again?

I remember my youngest sister telling of being in the hospital days before Da passed away and facing a major dilemma. Da had requested a back rub to alleviate some discomfort. Imagine Evelyn did not know how to approach her own father in his distress as she had never touched him before. She also had witnessed his displeasure in her misadventures down through the years and had borne the brunt of the odd cold shoulder or two. At least she was brave enough to go to the hospital. I was still seething from the effects of our ongoing feud. Da had long since let go but by the time he lifted the white flag high in the air for the last time, his stubborn gene was already trickling into my blood stream.

The youngest of my father's flock in her very late thirties stood in apprehension alongside the hospital bed afraid to massage his aching back, unaware of his pending demise. The end was about to bring a new beginning. It wasn't that she didn't want to do it. It was about having the wherewithal to reach out and comfort someone who was so unreachable all our lives. Suddenly he was giving the okay because he needed the contact not only for the relief of pain, but for the feeling of being loved. Did he, too, need a good old hug? I had the same quandary years before, as I was sent home from a counselling session to embrace my mother. It felt equally awkward and terrifying. I remember telling Mam what I was about to do in case I sent her over the edge and my sister Geraldine asking me if I was "nuts". Actually, she used a stronger word. Funny now looking back.

I only became natural at it when Mam got Alzheimer's as I was doing it for her then, not for my own benefit. I never got that chance with Da as I was well rooted in an impasse at the time, feeling shit about letting him down and equally angry at him for his inability to embrace me when I had fallen to my knees.

My fall from grace was cancelled out when he fell in love with the result of that particular fall, Lailah. She grabbed a hold on his heart strings at six months old in her rocky cot on my mother's kitchen floor. Lailah was barely three years of age when he had a massive heart attack. It was a few days after Da had asked for my sister's care in the hospital. Many bridges were about to be mended at the close of his life. It's ironic that Dad had the anxiety gene and made a sudden uncomplicated exit from this world. Mam had the calm gene and had to endure a long disquieting goodbye.

# The bliss gene

There was no surprise for me when the following article landed in my letter box from my sister, Miss France. At last, somebody somewhere had the balls to fling this particular cat out of its dusty old bag and I am not talking about my sister here.

*Those of us who don't have the natural benefit of the gene of bliss are more likely to be anxious and to self-medicate.*

*Chances are that everyone on this planet has experienced anxiety, that distinct sense of unease and foreboding. Most of us probably assume that anxiety has a psychological trigger. Yet clinicians have long known that there are plenty of people who experience anxiety in the absence of any danger or stress and haven't a clue why they feel distressed. Despite years of psychotherapy, many experience little or no relief. It's as if they suffer from a mental state that has no psychological origin or meaning, a notion that would seem heretical to many therapists, particularly psychoanalysts.*

*Recent neuroscience research explains why in part, this may be the case. For the first time, scientists have demonstrated that a genetic variation in the brain*

> *makes some people inherently less anxious, and more able to forget fearful and unpleasant experiences. This lucky genetic mutation produces higher levels of anandamide – the so called bliss molecule and our own natural marijuana – in our brains.*
>
> – Richard A. Friedman, The Feelgood Factor in *The New York Times*

I do believe today that my father, God rest his soul, and I carried a little more anxiety in our blood than most and a touch too little marijuana for our own liking. From my late twenties I tried therapy after therapy including an ocean of psychotherapy, hypnotherapy, acupuncture, hands-off, hands-on healing, ate up every self-help book written and finally settled with meditation which is a possible escape or anchor depending on the day I'm having. Although I am neither a neuroscientist nor an expert in any field, I had made the above conclusion long ago. I say many times that "Hope Floats" and will do until my end because I feel life might just lack its wonder without it. I also believe Da did brilliantly because Mam had enough bliss genes and the wisdom to sustain them both. She was the calm in all his storms, in all our storms.

I had many such similar discussions with my sisters down through the years about genetics and in particular my missing bits and pieces. I know what calm is because when I am lucky to reside in its loveliness I don't have to talk myself into doing a task or going to meetings or choosing which toilet paper to buy. It comes easy. I also feel at home at an event or in a crowd, smell roses while in bloom and see wonder in almost everything that moves.

But, but, but, when "Bliss" is out of my range no matter how much meditation or positive thinking I secure, I circle the floor, sweat profusely, go on tenterhooks for demands or requests to keep at bay, praying that the day will end swiftly so I can crawl under a quilt and hide, hoping upon hope that my tomorrow will bring with it glad tidings.

My father was just like me. He retreated into the boxroom sometimes for hours, sometimes for days when this happy gene was out on leave. Mam graciously served him there until the fog lifted and he remerged a new man. Like me on good days he could sense his tomatoes ripen in the glass-house without leaving the house and greet every visitor as if they had returned from Australia. The ordinary days were joyous for us both if we had nothing extra to deal with, but dare anyone throw a boulder in our paths on those blissless days. This is where and when my wise Mam knew not to add to or put anything extra on my Da's plate. She got the best of him as she did not judge his desire to be alone.

This acknowledgement of a possible missing bliss gene is a blessing for me because it is like any affliction: if you know what is going on, it is a little easier to accept. Most people will not know when the light at the end of my tunnel is dim. Blissless compatriots will repel each other when we happen to experience this misery on the same day. Just like my Da. He was not able for my anxiety, not because he had no love in his heart for me, but because it exasperated his own ill feeling at the time. He had no room on his shoulders on those days to carry an extra load. I did not understand him or myself until now and unfortunately after his demise. But I do know he is damn proud from the other side that I understood and felt my mother's darkness while she was terrorized and ridiculed by this heartless tormentor Alzheimer's. There is a possibility that my very own anxiety made me more compassionate and helpful for Mam during her end of life sentence.

Author John O'Donahue puts it nicely. "There is a strength that comes from the depths of our own darkness and vulnerability". I guess this strength may sometimes come from knowingness.

I had to learn to hold my mother's hand gently regardless of which side my gene scales dipped on her rough days and allow her into my cave so we could huddle together until the storm passed.

This is why I believe that my psychotherapist suggesting years before to go to me Da and allow him to shoulder some of my cares was unrealistic and unkind to both of us. In order to reach me Da on this level he would have to have had a few pints and a good kick of whiskey to gradually allow him mellow and realise I did not need his blood. I just needed the odd thumbs up, a good old hug of compassion and a box of spuds or two which he had in abundance.

# Considering nursing home care

I t's great to be independent. I know of people who were well capable of caring for a parent at home with Alzheimer's. Their loved one did not wander or miss a night's sleep. Most importantly, the home environment had stability and support.

I know the opposite too. The struggle for another such family was to the detriment of the Alzheimer's patient, for the person caring and for their home environment. The patient became increasingly aggressive as senses and memory deteriorated leaving the family living constantly on the edge.

Therefore one must assess each situation individually. With every condition there are varying degrees of need, Some people live on their own needing a carer to look in on  them daily to make sure they have supplies. And then there are the harrowing cases. Mam had become a danger to herself and to others. The decision in the end was nursing home care. It followed hospital care while she was recovering from the broken hip and wrist.

I sat amongst my shattered family members as we discussed options. With all my reserve I had to slam the door of shame firmly shut that night. I eventually forgave myself for agreeing. I did not know with all my being that it was the right thing to do.

I did not have the courage or wherewithal to stand up and shout, 'I can do this'. Neither did I have the stamina to face this condition head on in order for Mam to be cared for in a family environment. I remember looking at the devastation on my brother's face as we summed up all the horrors of this condition and the fact that none of us knew if we were equipped to deal with it. There was one blessing – Mam was going to start this next chapter directly from hospital. There was going to be an easing into nursing home care before she would realise that her life on the outside was over.

Do you tell your loved one that they are "losing their mind?" I don't know the answer. Did I feel I was a traitor who had abandoned their mother? Yes. Over and over again. Did I feel responsible for her broken heart and spirit? Yes. Did I feel I could have done better for my dear mother who carried out her role as a care-giver without complaint for over fifty years? Yes. Did all this punishment serve me in any way? No. It drained my energy and probably aged me by many years. I wondered if my siblings felt the same way. Like a broken marriage or pregnancy outside of a union, this shame is never discussed. It is just borne by the person carrying it. Such is my personality I had to give myself a good beating before I could become a valuable member of a team of carers.

As with any illness, once it lands on your door it seems like an epidemic. Suddenly, all types of stories come galloping towards you, relating to whatever health issue is current. I now have knowledge of the journeys of many who have Alzheimer's. Some are manageable. Some are harrowing.

I can say with clarity now that in the early stages some Alzheimer's patients lose the ability to read, write, watch TV, play cards or take part in activities. This causes immense boredom and frustration. Such was the case with Mam. Therefore it was important to have visitors on a regular basis to keep her memory alert for as long as possible in order to reduce feelings of isolation and boredom. Fortunately for our family, this was achievable as we are strong in numbers and lived in close proximity to the nursing home.

The journey with nursing home care for us had many benefits. We had a medical team on hand 24/7 and we had our night's sleep. Therefore, we had new energy, hope and spirit as we grew together in our challenges, misery and laughter. I was eventually able to put the insistent doubts and questions to rest and support this decision 100%. That is the best anyone of us can do. Worry never robs tomorrow of its sorrow, it only saps today of its strength.

There is a possibility that your loved one will reject the notion of a nursing home, leaving you feeling like a traitor and that you have failed them miserably. To compound these feelings, you may be met by a blank stare coupled with a look of desperation saying, "How could you betray me like this?" At this stage your loved one has no comprehension that their short term memory is retreating forever. They are gradually going to lose their mobility, become childlike and whether they are in care or at home they will feel vulnerable, lost and frustrated.

Try not to lose heart. Keep trucking along. Visits are necessary. Remember each visit with love, care and compassion, it makes the journey a bit more bearable.

I have memories of these visits in the early stages, feeling that I made no difference at all. But sometimes out of the blue Mam would soften and a little light might flicker in her spirit giving my self-worth a little lift and enough fuel to motor on, day by day.

Our openness to nursing home care intertwined with good family support gave us a new beginning. We did not hand over responsibility. We played a very important part in Mam's care with non-stop visits and taking her out for breaks until it became distressing for her because of mobility issues.

If you are beginning to open up to support, research until the cows come home and travel if necessary to a different location if the grass is greener. With an easy heart, visit your loved one as much as possible. Be a part of their new world, watch over them, think for them, tuck them in, sing with them, hold their hands and hug them without reservation. Let people support you. Most of all, take one day at a time and try not to be too hard on yourself.

# Unease

Kindness is a type of language that the deaf can hear and the blind can see. During our nursing home years we got to witness many staff members who watched over Mam with enormous compassion and professionalism. We were overwhelmed by that heaven-sent care.

There were also other times, although few and far between, when I had feelings of unease about lack of care. My instinct told me that something other than the complications and frustrations of this condition was amiss. These feelings may have been amplified by each change in Mam's condition, which came with a fragile vulnerability, loss of self and loss of mobility.

Without doubt, every institution or walk of life employs staff straight from the heavens. Sadly the odd bad apple exists. It would be naive to think otherwise. We do not live in a perfect world. I think some individuals outgrow their profession and stay in these jobs because of lack of choice, unemployment in the area, suitable location, agreeable hours, or a nearing retirement package. So many people may be educated but not all have integrity and compassion.

We are all human and have our bad days. A wonderful member of a medical team can be impatient, grumpy or dismissive through exhaustion or stress. But a genuine caring nature will immediately make amends and move forward with greater care.

There is a great need for wisdom and vision in addressing unease. Your loved one may just be fed up or have refused help simply because they want to be left alone. A member of staff might remind them of someone from their past. It may be a personality clash.

Have an open mind. Your loved one's rejection of a particular employee may be warranted. If you feel there is cause for concern, discuss it with someone you trust. Ask for another doctor, nurse or care assistant to tend your loved one. "Neither let the grass grow under your feet, nor throw the baby out with the bath water". Sometimes there may be a simple solution. It may be helpful to try and find, "if possible" something positive about this employee and point it out. Sometimes appreciation alone has the power to re-ignite care and an interest in a profession.

Three of my sisters in long-term employment agree that the gratitude and support they receive regularly from their respective employers keeps a continual skip in their steps and interest in their roles. At all times your loved one's care is paramount and your own sanity is crucial. You need to dig deep for all positive aspects of any situation or intuition. It might be worthwhile to find a way around the unrest.

Be conscious of how your relative reacts to their care. You do not know if they are being treated with enough patience behind closed doors. It is a fact of life that your loved one needs you in times of unrest to be their voice and to act on their behalf.

Even in the depths of the Alzheimer's tunnel, I felt my Mam was still a wise soul and knew her care. She knew also what lay beneath a façade. When a member of staff came to tend to her you could feel her ease or unease. If your instinct troubles you about a particular issue or carer and you feel it is much more than vulnerability caused by health issues, consider a wonderful saying my sister, Miss US,  passed on to me. "If there is doubt, there is no doubt".

# Chicken wings

Dinner at our home when we were kids was a riot. Mam wore these full wrap-around aprons with big pockets and little flowers. She was everyone's dream mother. She was the last to sit and the last to be served, by herself of course, because we did absolutely nothing but eat, chat, squeal and act the monkey.

There was always contentment especially when cabbage was on the menu. I mention this green enemy for John's sake only. That table was the heart of the family and remains so today in all our own houses but especially for me as I inherited Mam's kitchen table. Mam reached for our every requirement whether it was another fork or knife, another drink of water, the salt or the butter. She did everything bar chew it for us. Remember there were eleven of us, so this was a marathon day after day.

She was the last to sit and eat. She ate the chicken wings. I remember as a child wondering how she ate those gross things. It was a "magic pot". Everyone was fed. No one went without although there appeared little in it. She also produced these wonderful potato cakes out of the left-over potatoes on the top of the fuel cooker.

I never wanted to leave that table. It was the only place I felt safe and secure. To this day, I am always topping up and

I never allow myself the feeling of being empty or hungry. Today chicken wings are my favourite part of a chicken. Maybe Mam secretly knew the wings were the best part after all. The difference now is I eat them before I serve. When I realised Mam was never going to be cooking again, I took her battered old stew saucepan and the roasting dish. My brother-in-law took them to his workshop and plugged the holes in them. Not only does everything taste better out of these pans, but there is always enough to go around.

After Mam passed away, I woke early one morning with a longing for that homely feeling of her shaking down the cooker with gusto to get the day off to a start. The sensation of security and warmth that emanated from her kitchen was vital for us as children, although too often we took it for granted especially during our teenage years.

The realisation that we can only appreciate our parents putting their lives on the line for us after they depart is natural. As we shake down our own fuel burners and take up the dirty laundry strewn about in the wind, we now know that these tedious jobs will be our own children's memories of home when we pass away. This, in turn gives significance to the monotony of it all.

# Katie Daly

**M**am is now gone almost six months. It is a Saturday afternoon and I am sitting here eating lunch with Midlands Radio playing in the background. I guess if my adult children who are just now touring Australia came into my kitchen they would experience the feeling I got time and time again when I was a child in Mam's kitchen. The smell of potato cakes on the pan, the fire glowing in the hearth and the sound of old Irish songs. Heart-warming stuff. This one has just come on the radio, "Oh, come down from the mountain Katie Daly," reminding me of Da. He must have sung it when he was in good form. History is repeating itself.

A friend phoned last night to tell me his Mam is in a confused state. My heart is shattered as I know only too well how distressing it is to leave the nursing home when a parent has that look of bewilderment. You feel like such a traitor for leaving them knowing that they are lost and frightened. If only you could pick them up, take them home, wrap them in cotton wool, and replace their confused state of mind with one of security, comfort and peace.

It has just come to me why the song about Katie Daly rings a bell right now. This old song, alongside many others, may reignite familiar homely feelings when the Alzheimer's patient is lost and confused. To sing a song that takes the patient back to that warm feeling may help draw out a positive sensation and gently ease away the confusion for a little while.

This man may wonder if his mother knows who he is while in this state but I feel on some level just like Mam, a mother knows her care. Mam did not speak for months but when two photographs fell out of her prayer book onto her bed only weeks before she died, she automatically said her grandchildren's names without prompt. But after that, not another word.

My sister and I go social dancing every other weekend. I remember when I first found this wonderful therapy. Da had just passed away. It was a bubble of happy sentiment when a song such as The Galway Shawl, about Da's county and related to my childhood was played. Those tunes were magic at the time. They kept his essence alive for me and still do. Today I am still transported back in time by old Irish music. It flips me right back to my mother's kitchen and all those lovely feelings of home, remembering Mam or Da humming along in the background.

It is always a delight to watch the older dancers. I have been blessed to have been in the company of many elderly couples dancing the slow waltz. I have also observed countless times one particular man gently guide his wife (with Alzheimer's) onto the dance floor. It's a heavenly sight and an immensely positive sign that no matter what condition is inflicted on someone, dancing and music has a therapeutic effect. If Mam had not progressed so rapidly with Alzheimer's, it would have given us great pleasure to have taken her out dancing, knowing she would have just loved it.

# Lavender talcum powder

When I ran out of the shower this morning I had a yearning to find my long-lost lavender talcum powder. I remember regretting not buying many more of these little containers in the euro saver shop because of its smooth natural fragrance.

You know the story. Some purchases, even though described one way, may turn out to be completely different. This one surprisingly was the real deal. As I picked up the container I immediately thought of Mam and the reason it had been hidden away for so long. I got fed up hoovering the tiled floors constantly until I got clever and removed the powder.

When Alzheimer's makes it presence felt, after a few near misses, the fire guard is resurrected, the kitchen devil replaced promptly with a potato peeler, non-slip mats are put in place and the talcum powder is history.

This takes me back to Lailah, approximately six years of age at the time. I had removed the powder without explaining to her. We parents do not always verbalise; we just act when a new realisation dawns. Lailah loved plastering her body with powder after her bath. When she discovered it was missing, she ran to the shower room to rummage in the storage press. I realised what she was at and screamed, "Do not use the powder". But she pleaded and I gave in.

I was probably preparing dinner or distracted with some other household duty, expecting Lailah to have caution when she was just a little child full of the magic of her carefree world. This was the rock I was about to perish on. My mother had done a good job of imprinting the words on my soul, "If only for peace sake, give in". She did not say, prepare, pre-empt or think ahead girl. Ha! You see, just like me, Mam did not explain much either. I sent Lailah off to my bedroom telling her to stand on the bed while applying the powder thinking even if she overdid it, dusting off a bed cover would be easier than Hoovering and washing a slippery floor. I made her promise to use just a little powder, still not taking the time to explain why it needed to be removed in the first place which in hindsight may have saved me an evening's work.

Minutes later Lailah heard me answer the front door to her older sister. She immediately called her into the bedroom to say hello. Then Sarah came to the kitchen looking bewildered and said, "Mam do you realise what Lailah is doing in your bedroom". I said, "Yes of course, I gave her permission to use the powder". Sarah's immediate response was, "It may be a good idea to check in on her". I ran into the room not thinking, struggling to keep my balance when my feet hit the bedroom floor. Jesus, Mary and Joseph, the room was like a building site. I could hardly see the child through the fog. She had probably started out small with good intention but got more adventurous, continued to shake the powder and then of course for better effect started to jump up and down on the bed. This energy of course helped the powder to disperse, rise into the air and land gently covering all surfaces it met.

It is a pity, I did not think at the time to take a photograph. All the commotion from coming and going left an image one might witness at Christmas time, a pathway decorated with shoe prints after a fall of snow. I spent that entire evening shaking out sheets and bedclothes, sweeping, Hoovering and washing floors.

As time moves on and Mam's memory fades, a word, a song, a place or an item such as the little box of talcum powder still has the ability to stop me in my tracks for a moment and reflect. A little jolt back in time now and again is normal.

# Stone monuments

What you leave behind is not what is engraved on stone monuments, but what is woven into the lives of others.

I have read this sentence many times, a quote from my mother's day-by-day book, which accompanied her prayer book on the dressing table in the nursing home. I bet anyone who sat at her bedside read that little book full of quotes and inspirational stories. Reading this one reminds me of my mother, a wonderful doctor and many other great souls who took my hands with tender loving care at a dark time in my life and pulled me towards the light.

My publisher asked me why I had the desire to write this book. The reason is clear: we were blessed to come from a frugal existence and to have had a great teacher, my mother. She taught us morality, the greatest gift one can give. I walked and stumbled through life not knowing my greatness but somehow was blessed to encounter other people along my path to point this truth out and the reason for it. I hope that the following story will explain why I am determined to keep plugging away.

I am going back almost eleven years to the day of my first appointment with an absolute angel, a counsellor, wise one, seer, mother earth and last, but not least, doctor. People are impressed by the Master's degrees lining the offices of our professionals. They would be better served to seek out, at all costs, the characteristics above. Maybe they should view those plaques with the intention to seek out "A Master's in Empathy", which I believe may only be acquired from the gods. It is the script with the golden hue emanating. Believe me there is a hell of a lot more healing from a compassionate heart, a loving tone or a kind deed than from writing out a prescription.

I did not know if I was taking a turn in the right direction the day I met this great lady. I was in too much physical, emotional and mental pain to be tuned in or thinking clearly. I had been in an accident, which left me with frozen shoulder accompanied by excruciating back pain and to top it all pregnant outside of a union at forty years of age. I had no choice but to make the decision to close my business leaving me without an income which, in turn, left me scrambling with an insurance company who were never going to honour our agreement.

Now some may think my situation may not seem like such a big deal, but I was feeling downright crushed at the thoughts of telling my teenage son and daughter that I was carrying a child when I was busy up to this point preaching safe sex. Shame. Not to mind the thoughts of facing my poor father who had already shined his gun once or twice over the years for my benefit. I guess I had caused a stir too many before this point. He was slow to accept the disgrace I had brought to his door from my divorce ten years earlier. In fairness, bless his heart, he was just beginning to relax his grip on the trigger.

Going back to the doctor's surgery, Sarah had warned me that I would have a long wait on the morning of my first appointment. She was not exaggerating. My sister bombarded me with text after text, encouraging me not to abandon ship and ensuring me with conviction that this doctor had the ability to save my life. Was this appointment worth the wait? I might as well have walked into my mother's kitchen. I instantly felt the weight of the world lift and began to wonder what led me there in the first place. All pain and anxiety seemed to slip magically away as I was placed gently in a cocoon of kindness. Instantly, this beautiful lady filled me with hope after hearing my story telling me I had nothing to worry about. She said with knowingness that I was carrying a little angel and that given time and right therapy my shoulder and back would heal. She also informed me that I was blessed to have a very "strong family" behind me as she knew my sisters, whom she felt were the salt of the earth.

She warned me to give all naysayers a wide berth and to tell the world this child was planned and sent straight from the gods. Before I left, she took my two hands in hers and said that I would tell her on my next appointment that all was well. I still remember leaving that office with a little skip in my step, feeling I could handle just about anything with my renewed spirit.

I then went along as advised to see the recommended gynaecologist. Fortunately for me, this man was also hand-picked from heaven. He immediately informed me that he had received a call from my new doctor requesting that I be treated with great care as there was a very important angel about to enter the world. Without hesitation, he also said that there was a special reason for this new arrival which would reveal itself in time. Imagine how enamoured I felt. After just one visit my new doctor took the time to contact this man personally in order to make my journey lighter. Could they between them see why this child was to enter my world? It was beyond comprehension.

The pregnancy was tortuous with back pain and reflux. Somehow I was dragged forward by an invisible force of love. My family did indeed run on board my sinking ship to keep it afloat. They tenderly guided it to dry land, while many other helping hands slipped in quietly behind me and made it possible for me to face each day. My sister-in-law spent countless evenings after she ended her day's work massaging my shoulder as I could not take the pain medication while pregnant.

Lailah, my shiny new "angelic blessing", entered this world puffing smoke just like me Da, kicking and screaming. She did not sleep through the night until she was five years of age after the removal of her tonsil and adenoids. These oversized organs had caused her recurring infections and difficulty sleeping.

I can tell you I questioned that word angel once or twice during those years and since. However, this doctor would reappear out of thin air again and again after Lailah's birth, always when I was on my knees feeling that I could not go on. I remember being sent to a health centre at Christmas-time with Lailah, then four, to be greeted once again by outstretched hands as if she was personally waiting for the child. She had this wondrous way with all patients, young or old. For us two sorrowful souls after many sleepless nights it was always about the greeting we received accompanied by a knowing smile. Imagine this doctor was giving up her Christmas to make ours and many others. This is not duty, it is care beyond words. Now I know many doctors give of their time during the festive season but how many do it with such warmth and compassion?

Mother Theresa put it beautifully: "We should not set out to do great things, just small things with great love."

I was sent out of this doctor's surgery after that very first appointment with new hope, to gather my thoughts and put things into perspective, which led me to my mother's cosy kitchen. This little haven was the only place on earth where I knew the big bad wolf could not get me.

My mother was the queen of calm. When I told her there was another grandchild on the way, she sat on a chair across from me and said that it was the best news she had heard in such a long time. Imagine my mother never once enquired who or where was the father figure for this blessing. She looked at me as if I had given her the most important news in the world, repeating sweetly that I was truly blessed as tears of joy ran down her cheeks. Little did Mam know that in time this little angel was to become a companion for her when Alzheimer's came knocking on her door some years later. Ironically, the gynaecologist told me a similar story about his parents having a child later in life and the blessings that followed as a result.

It only took two years for my back to heal, about the same amount of time it took for me Da to forgive me "once again" for falling off his tight rope and he actually found a place in his heart for Lailah. It is funny now, as I look back and see him in my mind's eye running to hide, as my car entered his driveway while I was pregnant. Not one bit amusing at the time. It would have given me the greatest pleasure to have sat with him in the heavens on a great big fluffy cloud years later to view Lailah caring for Mam in the early stages before Alzheimer's.

I have many sweet memories of Lailah reading, painting, drawing and fetching Mam a blanket or a Rosary beads during that time. I remember only too well, during the attempted escape period, Mam asking Lailah repeatedly could she sleep in her bedroom. Or, eventually as a compromise, would the child stay in the nursing home as her companion. Bittersweet memories. I guess this little angel came into our world for more reasons than one. The rest has yet to unfold.

There are many explanations for writing this book. First of all I want to shine the light on my Mam, my well-grounded family and friends, and last but not least a wonderful doctor.

To dismiss or to move forward without taking account or acknowledging these wonderful hearts that have the ability to lift the darkness would be wrong and would contradict our blessed beginnings.

My Mam died without knowing her greatness. Therefore the ones who still reside on this earth bestowed with the art of weaving hope into the hearts of others should be acknowledged. I guess to let my mother's world end in darkness without reaching for the stars would be a sin. This is why I want the journey with Alzheimer's recorded. Mam did not go to college and did not have a string of capital letters after her name. She had much much more; she had an endless supply of light, love and perseverance.

My mother left behind eleven adult children, each with the ability to weave their own nests. We are old and wise enough now to have encountered many homes without this necessary foundation. Therefore, without doubt, we were privileged that we had two parents who believed in the importance of a unit.

Second of all there is nothing physical left. Mam and Da and even our little cottage on the hill have long since gone. This book for our family alone is a record or memory of two ordinary people who strived to remain honest and simple leaving behind their care. My core intention is to capture some of my parents' values and characteristics that thankfully live on in our bloodline.

I live in hope that by sharing this book with the world it may be of help to others walking the trying road of Alzheimer's. It might fight some of the loneliness and answer some of the baffling questions. It might give a little insight or direction, even if it leads to acceptance alone, knowing that our family had not a clue what to do as we just moved forward with the intention of finding a way, any way, day by day. Thankfully we made it to the finish line. Thankfully we are still a unit, still intact.

# Once is not enough

My brave sister Geraldine who said occasionally that once is more than enough, bit the proverbial bullet and married for a second time. Mercifully she is still happily married after five weeks and a few days. We live in hope in the happy ever after. Geraldine is like the cartoon character Tigger or is it Eeyore? She is the one that bounces back. Life would be very dull if you only lived it once.

There is no doubt that she had my mother's blessing and energy on the day. It was like the whole family appeared unusually sedated. To use the word "calm" to describe the occasion would be an understatement. The ceremony and after-party were truly scattered with angel dust. Even the clouds disappeared and the sun shone over the wedding guests for the entire event. Maybe this was a gift from the gods for Geraldine, for being an anchor for my parents. Didn't they survive eleven children and fifty years of a marital whirlwind?

Yes, there is no doubt Geraldine was mysteriously granted more enchantment than any wishful person could imagine. The dresses, church, music, blessings, guests and party jelled together effortlessly like something dropped out of a fairy tale. The after-party was originally planned for my brother's house but when immediate families were counted it felt unrealistic to try squeezing this bunch in and the golf club opened its doors willingly. Out of a tiny budget emerged a ceremony fit for royalty. It was captivating. Imagine being slightly tipsy without the help of alcohol and loving each moment and each guest. Maybe my sister, Mary, went to town on the Bailey's Irish Cream while making the wedding cake. Maybe that's what softened the guests.

Life goes on after our parents exit the physical world and our units get restructured. I think it gets better because we begin to appreciate our time and our care, we find the lighter side of our personalities or characters, instead of leaning towards perfection, we become less judgmental. Maybe at fifty two my sister is better able for a real marriage. With the benefit of hindsight she now has the ability to keep the spirit of a union above water and splash its delights among others. Geraldine is an example of the sayings, "falling down is never a problem as long as you have the strength to get back up" and "kick the dust off while moving forward with conviction and hope".

I slipped this note into my brother-in-law to be's pocket after I had repaired his wedding suit hem.

> *John – this is a little note to let you know in advance that you have already been more than welcome into our family and lives. I have been moved joyously in so many ways since you approached our table in The Well, the night the gods, (Inc. sweet little cupid), decided that yourself and Ger were to fall in love, dance, walk, talk, jive, explore, eat, pray, laugh, compare notes, argue points, lift each other's hearts and spirits on grey days and smell the roses on lighter ones.*

*Those few years seem like fleeting moments because they carried so much joy, hope, unity and blessings. You are a wonderful man and we all know without a doubt that Geraldine, our rock, has shifted us all over a bit on her family tree to make room for another great soul, having you in our world does not in any way take away from Geraldine's relationship with us because she now has so much more to give, I guess that's what two wonderful hearts coming together amount to.*

*Now to put the icing on the cake, we are also blessed to know you are taking Geraldine's hand with courage and care and walking down the unpredictable road of marriage with it peaks and valleys, the only thing you are guaranteed is that you have all of us firmly behind you wishing and praying that every day will be filled with wonder and grace and each mountain climb easier with the knowledge you are in the hands of a great great lady, our loyal and steadfast sister, aunt, mother and friend.*

*Love Anne and family*

*To: Geraldine & John & her children*

# The lady with the yellow cardigan

I took myself off to the supermarket to purchase food for Sunday dinner. Geraldine was coming home from her honeymoon. It was evening time and I was in tip top form as it was the end of one of those wonderful days where everything fell smoothly into place. We were all still glowing from the wedding the weekend before and looking forward to a get together to view photographs.

While entering the supermarket I glimpsed an elderly lady with a soft yellow cardigan, blue dress and a walking cane. Minding my own business, I collected a trolley and then busied myself filling it. Just as I was about to enter the veg section there she was waiting for me, her gentle eyes reaching right into my soul. I opened my mouth to greet her but nothing emerged as suddenly I felt my chest contract, probably from the lack of oxygen. She stole my breath away.

All I know for sure, in those moments that followed there was nobody else in the world, both of us locked in a deep gaze. I might have believed that I had died and gone to Heaven but for the fact that I was surrounded by big shelves stacked with food and the bustle of trollies whizzing by. I was transformed from a happy shopper to an inconsolable mess.

I sobbed uncontrollably while this beautiful 94-year-old lady gently held me in her arms and drew my longing into her heart with compassion. What longing you might well ask as I have already explained that I had clearly moved on and the effects of my mother's passing had long since dissolved into the ether. Then out of the blue this lady gently voiced the words "your Mammy". Feeling like a complete fraud I tried earnestly to explain that Mam had passed way over two years ago but as I prised myself from her arms I found a replica of my mother and just like Mam, with a kind gesture she graciously offered the warmest little nod. Wow, more tears.

At this stage this beautiful lady's daughters had come to her rescue and acknowledged that the sighting of their Mam was bound to stir up emotion for anyone who had lost a parent. In due course I had no choice but to hand this lady back into the care of her daughters She was a blessed one graced with good physical and mental health, well into her nineties. I reluctantly walked away with a cloud of sadness sitting on my shoulders and threw some veg carelessly into the trolley as I tried to compose myself.

I dragged myself to the checkout still sobbing, my trolley, daughter and sister in tow; well I could not abandon the basket of food or my guests for dinner the following day would suffer. Deep down inside I knew these particular wolves would not be impressed with empty plates. Another grief story was never going to cut it. The tears continued to flow as I left the supermarket, went through the busy town and deep into the countryside until eventually the sorrow dissolved. I was pleased to greet my guests with a heart light as a feather the following day. The show must go on.

There is little doubt that Mam's spirit had been with us the week before as we gathered for Geraldine's wedding. I guess unknown to us her remaining siblings, her energy helped set the stage for the odd bit of reminiscence. It was no accident that I ran into Mam's carbon copy in the supermarket a week later just before her memory was about to be laid to rest once again.

I remember one of our famous country and western stars telling a story of going into a petrol station after his Mam passed and being rooted to the spot at the sight of an elderly lady standing near the checkout. He was so attacked by grief that he left the shop without paying for the petrol which he had just pumped. I guess this payment was settled at a later date. We are such funny creatures, us humans.

# Our guru

Poll Mary Pender was the glue that held an entire community of relations and friends together. Poll was Mam's and Dad's mediator. She had a gift. She knew naturally when to step in or when to step down to save an argument. Once a storm was about to brew in the early years she would come to our kitchen table with conviction. She spoke out clearly and honestly when my father would not listen to reason.

The cavalry, namely Poll, had to be called in at these times when it seemed that me Da was clearly on the edge of blowing an almighty fuse and causing havoc in our calm world. Poll told us mischievously on her death bed that Mam kicked her good and hard under the table during one of these meetings to indicate that she was on the right track. Instead however, Poll took it as a reason to shut up for fear of being a little too hard on Dad.

This lady was articulate and fair, having a natural ability to put things into perspective and because of this my father had respect for her and did not ban her entirely from our home.

There were no phones or cars back then. When a dilemma needed sorting, the eldest scurried up and down the road on bikes delivering notes indicating that a meeting was necessary. Mam obviously vented all arduous cares to Poll.

These smart ladies told my father little, allowing him the freedom to get on with the job of being a provider without extra baggage.

Poll's wisdom and conviction as me Mam's guru saved my brothers many times when accused in the wrong as teenagers. The door always remained slightly ajar because of Poll's leading light even for us girls when boldly falling off the tight rope time and time again.

Poll had two fine sons and a pleasing husband John, never far from his kitchen stove after finishing a day's work. That left her at ease to run, trot and gallop to save the world. Mam had eleven little chicks in tow, and although Dad steadfastly kept a roof over our heads, he was little help in dealing with the antics of child-rearing. Mam was ultimately tied to the kitchen sink until we were all adults and building our own nests.

Even as a very small child, I knew Poll's importance in our world and I admired her tremendously. Just like with our own Mam I had no idea of the true extent of her greatness until she passed away. Imagine, I thought we were the chosen few she set out to shelter from life's storms. I was swiftly enlightened by sympathisers at her wake in their enchant-ing little cottage with its half door. Clearly, Poll's stamina had the ability to extend itself upwards and outwards to many homes. She was prepared at all times to lift one depleted spirit after another and stand firmly behind the misunderstood.

She was a mischief-maker. Poll had the ability to make a cat laugh right up to her last breath, boldly pretending to be dead in the bed to crack us up.

Her wonderful character and spirit remained unbroken, although her dwindling independence eventually started to eke away her appetite for living. After lovingly holding John's hand for a week before he passed, without reservation she announced that she was more than ready to take leave of this world and join her companion in the heavens. She was buried alongside John a few weeks later.

Poll was the final piece of my mother's jigsaw, a wonderful courageous and fair friend who in life was a magic cushion for many a soft landing.

An email from Ms South of France was read after Poll's funeral:

> Her passion for life was contagious. Poll was the life and soul of a never-ending party others call life. A fixture in my world since the day I opened my eyes … She lived a few houses over from us in the early days, a 25 minute walk. I shared with her all the magic moments reserved for Grandparents. I'd save money from cleaning Mrs Carter's house on Saturdays. Using the savings and winnings from Bingo games, I scraped enough money to buy my first bike. Arriving at her house, Poll reacted with the exuberance of a squealing pig being fed, "look at you not two hands higher than a duck on your new bike". The bike was a little big for me. Poll slipped me a few bob, a shilling in those days, for my first Communion and Confirmation.
>
> Years later, she drove me to my first job which looking back might have been scary for her leaving the country roads to find a mansion in the Dublin Hills. I was a nanny for a well to do family in 1976.

*There are two types of comedians, natural and unnatural. The unnatural get a laugh every other joke. But Poll was a natural. She had a gift. Her hilarity always upended downfalls, tripled celebratory moments and any reason to see a funny side was a good reason.*

*She came to visit me once in London. I took her to a car boot sale in a big field. She was like a kid in a toy shop. Her eyes lit up at all the bargains. She saw a china teacup and saucer with yellow flowers. The owner wrapped it carefully in newspaper for Poll to add to her interesting china cabinet back home. She then spotted a rug with a delicate weave. I marvelled at her exhilaration, watching her roll up that rug to take on a plane home. Made me smile.*

*When she died this week I found myself crying and laughing in turn. I went to the ocean and put some Lavender in the sea to celebrate her rich contribution to my life and to many others. Live one life – run like you are on fire to live your wildest dreams. That was our Poll.*

# Hope

Today she has a pink glow on her cheeks and is in a beautiful peaceful place while Geraldine and Sarah and I sit by her bedside eating chocolate and having a laugh. Yes, we offered Mam chocolate but she would not open her mouth. Instead she reached out for some and like a curious child held it between her fingers watching it melt.

This journey with a parent, friend or sibling facing the onset of Alzheimer's is one hard sentence with its craziness, terror, loneliness, adjustments, heartbreak, losses, pain and readjustments. Thankfully, it also has its rewards, lessons, its drawing out of love, patience, perseverance, loyalty, core values, stability, wisdom, support, togetherness, fun, hugs, affection, love and amazing growth.

Right now, I am so glad that I hugged Mam to bits when she sat in the dayroom of the nursing home because those hugs are no more. I am also glad I took off my shoes and got into bed beside her when I did not know what else to do as tears of frustration ran down her face. Those times are no more.

We did not come from a huggy, affectionate family background and we certainly did not know how to express ourselves or what to do with emotional outbursts. This unnvited condition, Alzheimer's, opened a new door or two along the way. I will always remember the first hug in the dayroom. I felt Mam needed to feel someone's care as her sad demeanour changed immediately.

My kind-hearted mother knew how I struggled with her condition. No matter how hard I tried I could not wish it away on the very dark days. I remember her first fall in the nursing home. Mam was found on the floor in the shower room with a little gash on her forehead. I was told this news as I sat beside her in the dayroom and try as I might I was unable to stop myself from crying.

I had this vision of her lying alone on the floor helpless in a strange room. Her tears dried up the moment she witnessed my distress and concern. I felt I could not protect her. Nobody could. She was in the safest environment possible and yet these things were going to happen. Mam was now dependent on a Zimmer for support and balance as there was a possibility of weakness and disorientation. Sometimes she tried to go it alone without an aid leaving herself vulnerable. It's amazing that we come into this world needing support and assistance and leave it the same way when old age or Alzheimer's comes knocking. This may be a fact of life but knowing it logically does not take away the want for it to be different.

At the beginning I was angry, sad and miserable. I did not think it possible to find a lighter side to all of this. But there is the art of acceptance. It is not something you get. It is something you must grow into. There is no magic wand but there is a strength that appears from the depths of our being so that we have the courage to take it one step at a time.

Writing this book has given me the opportunity to re-capture the good times and some beautiful memories of my mother's character while she was well and an active member of our family and community.

Hope is that little flicker of light in your soul that sparkles when it seems all is lost.

I hope her story will help others similarly affected to not feel so alone. I hope it will ease the desperation when presented with the diagnosis, Alzheimer's.